بسم الله الرحمن الرحيم

Mansell Islamic Studies

Series editor *Ziauddin Sardar*

£25.00
29

GLOSSARY OF ISLAMIC ECONOMICS

Muhammad Akram Khan

MANSELL

LONDON AND NEW YORK

First published 1990 by **Mansell Publishing Limited**
A Cassell imprint
Artillery House, Artillery Row, London SW1P 1RT, England
125 East 23rd Street, Suite 300, New York 10010, U.S.A.

British Library Cataloguing in Publication Data

Khan, Muhammad Akram
Glossary of Islamic economics.—(Mansell Islamic Studies)
1. Islamic, Economic
I. Title
330'.0917'671

ISBN 0-7201-2042-X

Library of Congress Cataloging in Publication Data

Khan, Muhammad Akram.
Glossary of Islamic economics / Muhammad Akram Khan.
p. cm.—(Mansell Islamic studies)
ISBN 0-7201-2042-X
1. Economics—Dictionaries—Arabic. 2. Economics—Religious aspects—Islam—Dictionaries—Arabic. 3. Arabic language—Dictionaries—English. I. Title. II. Series.
HB61.K46 1990
330'.03—dc20

89-13185
CIP

Printed and bound in Great Britain by
Biddles Ltd, Guildford and King's Lynn

Contents

Preface

This glossary has a short history. The need for it arose out of my own inadequacy in understanding the literature on Islamic economics. I have had a fascination for Islamic economics since 1963, and by 1970 I had almost decided that I would devote my life to developing this subject as an independent branch of knowledge. But I felt that in the absence of a commonly understood terminology, it was not possible to understand and communicate in the subject. I felt that, like myself, a large number of young graduates from the Western system of education have the desire and potential to contribute to the development of this subject, but they are not equipped properly with traditional Islamic knowledge. They do not have direct access to the primary sources of Islam. They need to be provided with a broad, general and precise explanation of the technical terms which they come across in the literature on Islamic economics. It is in response to the need of this group that this book has been written.

Technical terms are a *sine qua non* for the development of an academic discipline, providing a means for precise and economic communication. This book is an effort to present an inventory of technical terms used in Islamic economics, which it is hoped will lead this infant discipline a few steps further on the road to its recognition as a branch of knowledge.

Another objective for writing this book is to develop a better communication with Western scholars, economists and bankers, who have recently shown a keen interest in Islamic economics. This book, I hope, will provide them with a convenient means to understand (and even to use) the technical terms often applied in the literature.

I have been compiling over the past sixteen years the various terms used in the literature on Islamic economics. At times I was not quite sure whether a writer was using a particular phrase as a technical term or was just applying an Arabic expression. In the absence of a standard lexicographical work on Islamic economics I had to use my own judgement. Therefore, whatever terms appear in this compilation have my subjective bias about their being technical terms. In formulating this judgement, however, I have often relied on whether a word was being used in its plain lexicographical meaning or to mean something different. In the latter case I have often selected a phrase rather than a single word.

A large number of terms used are from legal sources, but I have tried to avoid, as far as possible, the adoption of any particular juridical point of view so as not to pre-empt the judgement of future researchers. Therefore, the technical terms give a general meaning and not the legal position in respect of each word.

Most of the terms are from the Arabic, since the primary sources of Islamic economics are in that language. However, due to a flurry of recent research publications in Urdu and English, I have also included technical terms from literature in those languages as well as some terms of Turkish or Persian origin. The Arabic words have been transliterated into English on the assumption that they cannot be adequately translated into English. I have also provided the Arabic version of these terms with the main entries.

A large number of entries in this glossary are *fiqh* terms, some of which are out-of-date. However, they have been included in the hope that students of Islamic economic history may be able to benefit from them.

The sources for this book are innumerable. It is not possible for me to recall where I picked up each particular term during the last sixteen years. However, I have relied on the following lexicographical works for checking the accuracy of the meanings:

Al-'Asfahani, al-Raghib, *Mu'jam Mufradat 'Alfaz al-Qur'an*. Beirut: Dar al-Katib al-'Arabi, 1392 A.H.

'Ibn al-'Athir, Majd al-Din Abu al-Sa'adat, *al-Nahayah fi Gharib al-Hadith wal 'Athar*. Beirut: Dar al-Turath al-a'Arabi, 1963 (5 vols.).

Qal'aji, M. Rawwas and H.S. Qunaibi, *Mu'jam Lughah al-Fuqaha*. Beirut: Dar al-Nafaes, 1985.

Lane, E.W., *An Arabic-English Lexicon*. London: Barley Brothers, 1955–6 (8 vols.).

Cowan, J.M., *A Dictionary of Modern Written Arabic*. London: Macdonald Evans, 1974.

My thanks are due to innumerable scholars and writers on Islamic economics, who provided me the source material for this book, but they are too many to be thanked individually. I must also express my deep gratitude to my wife, Aquila, and to my children, Junaid, Noori, Asma and Amna, who spared me during all the years I was working on this project.

Transliteration of Arabic Words and Names

ا	a consonantal sound	ط	ṭ
ء	a consonantal sound	ظ	ẓ
ا	ā long vowel	ع	' inverted apostrophe
ب	b	غ	gh
ت	t	ف	f
ث	th	ق	q
ج	j	ک	k
ح	ḥ	ل	l
خ	kh	م	m
د	d	ن	n
ذ	dh	ه	h
ر	r	و	w consonant
ز	z	و	u long vowel
س	s	و	au diphthong
ش	sh	ى	y consonant
ص	ṣ	ى	ī long vowel
ض	ḍ	ى	ai dipthong

Glossary

A

al-ʾadadīyyāt (العدديات)
Things which are sold by units, such as fruit.

al-ʿadl (العدل)
Lit: straightness, justice, fairness, equitableness. *Tech* (consists of two elements): first, that a sort of balance and proportion should be maintained between the people with respect to their rights; second, that every one's due share should be conscientiously rendered to that person. What justice (*adl*) really demands is balance and proportion, rather than equality in the rights of citizenship. In certain respects, equality is quite contrary to justice, such as in the moral and social equality between parents and their children, or in the equality of remuneration between those doing higher services and those not so eminently engaged. What Allah has ordained is proportion and balance in the equality of rights. This order requires that to every person should be honestly rendered all moral, social, economic, legal, political and civil rights. *Al-adl* is a mother virtue in a Muslim society. Individuals and society as a whole have been exhorted to observe justice in all their dealings. *Ant*: *al-zulm*, which is to deprive one of one's rightful and just share.

al-ʿafaf (العفاف)
Lit: abstinence, virtuousness, decency, honesty. *Tech*: satisfac-

tion with the little one may have to the extent that one appears rich. *Quran* 2:273.

African Arabian Islamic Bank (AAIB)
An international bank registered in the Bahamas and entirely owned by private Muslim individuals, the bank claims to conduct its operations on the basis of the Shariah. It offers services in syndicated interest-free loans, international investment, technology transfer, trade, commodities and currency trade and development funding. Perhaps the most prestigious of the bank's recent (1984) involvements is the multimillion-dollar monorail scheme linking Calgary to Edmonton (Canada). Similarly, the bank is arranging financial and trading services for Powell Chemicals of the United States for Arabian Express Card—the first consumer discount and travel protection card in the Arab World—and for various other activities, such as gold and diamond mining in West Africa, wind-mill technology in Salt Lake city and tar-sand technology in Canada.

al-ʿafw **(العفو)**
Lit: surplus. *Tech*: The expression appears in the Quran (2:219), wherein people have been instructed to spend in the cause of Allah whatever is over and above their needs. Some people have also applied the concept of *al-afw* to the canons of taxation in the Islamic economy. According to them, the Islamic state should tax people on the income or wealth which is over and above the basic needs of individuals.

Agreement for Promotion, Protection and Guarantee of Investments among Member States of the Islamic Conference
Initiated by Saudi Arabia in 1981 to supplement and make firm the 1977 General Agreement among OIC countries, it primarily relates to liberalization of capital movements and protection of direct investments by member states.

'aḥādīth al-mu'āmalah (أحاديث المعاملة)
Traditions of the Prophet relating to the Khaibar lands which he gave back to the Jews for cultivation on half share of the produce.

al-'ain (العين)
Relating to the law of *zakat*, originally meaning gold and silver, now also applicable to coins, currency notes, demand deposits, time deposits and any other form in which money may be held. The word has several other meanings in *fiqh* in general.

al-'ajīr al-khāṣṣ (الأجير الخاص)
Lit: Specific worker. *Tech*: A fulltime worker who agrees to perform a certain duty for one employer exclusively; for example, a watchman, who sells his time exclusively to his employer.

al-'ajīr al-mushtarak (الأجير المشترك)
Lit: Shared worker. *Tech*: A worker or craftsman who does not deserve his wage until he performs the duty assigned to him; for example, a washerman, a dyer or a carpenter. Such craftsmen do not sell the whole of their time; instead, they agree to perform certain functions for certain wages. They accept to perform these functions but not exclusively for any particular person. Their time is shared by all those persons who want them to perform these functions.

al-'ajr al-mithl (الأجر المثل)
Wages prevalent in the market for a certain service.

al-'akarah (الأكره)
Historically, peasants who held no fixed leases and were mostly landless day labourers.

'akl bil bātil (أكل بالباطل)
Lit: Eating someone else's property unjustifiably. *Tech*: It is the Quranic expression for unlawful acquisition of wealth such as *riba*, bribery and usurpation of orphan's wealth, etc.

'akl al-suḥt (أكل السحت)
Lit: Acquiring illegal property. *Tech*: Quranic term for bribery, especially to accept gifts for distorting divine guidance.

al-'amanah (الأمانة)
Lit: Reliability, trustworthiness, loyalty, honesty. *Tech*: An important value of Islamic society in mutual dealings. It also refers to deposits in trust. A person may hold a property in trust for another, sometimes by express contract and sometimes by implication of a contract.

al-Ameen Islamic Financial and Investment Corporation (India) Limited
Incorporated on 12 April 1984 in Karnatak (India), it has four branches, authorized capital of Rs.10 million. Paid-up capital, Rs.0.5 million.

al-'āmil (العامل)
In a contract of *mudarabah*, the person who acts as entrepreneur. Also used for a collector of *zakat*.

'āmil al fai' (عامل الفیء)
The official appointed to collect *jizyah* and *kharaj*, to lease *fai* land and superintend its cultivation. The *amil* would receive payment for his services from out of the revenue collected by him. He was not authorized to spend the revenue collected by him without permission.

al-'amilīn (العاملین)
Used in the law of *zakat* for tax-collectors, it includes all such officials as collectors, clerks, scribes, distributors, store-keepers, accountants, etc.

al-'amīn al-'āmm (الأمین العام)
A person who holds in trust property of another person, possession of which has been passed on to the trustee by the owner himself, but the principal objective of transfer is not safe

custody. For example, a tenant who hires a house or a *mudarib* in a contract of *mudarabah*, etc.

al-ʾamīn al-khāṣṣ (الأمين الخاص)
A person who holds in trust property of another person with the principal objective of safe-custody.

al-ʿamir (العامر)
Lit: Inhabited or cultivated land. *Tech*: A land belonged to a people collectively, such as a path, a canal or a river. Nobody can claim ownership of these lands except with the express permission of these people. See *al-mawat*.

al-ʾamwāl (الأموال)
See *al-mal*.

al-ʾamwāl al-fāḍilah (الأموال الفاضلة)
Lit: Miscellaneous receipts. *Tech*: Miscellaneous receipts of the *bait al-mal*. It was a regular head of account in the *bait al-mal* of the caliph and consisted of such receipts as *luqatah*, property of the heirless or properties of persons who had fled from the Islamic state.

al-ʾamwāl al-ribawiyyah (الأموال الربوية)
It connotes six items on which *riba al-fadl* arises: gold, silver, dates, wheat, salt and barley. Their exchange has been conditional with equality in weight and measure and simultaneous transfer of possession, failing which it would involve *riba al-fadl*. It has been held by some jurists that *riba al-fadl* arises only in respect of these six articles, but others have included such other articles as well which could be accepted as being similar to these six.

al-ʾanfāl (sing. al-nafl) (الأنفال)
Lit: An accretion or addition received beyond one's due. *Tech*: Spoils of war, signifying that they are incidental accessions above and beyond anything that a *mujahid* is entitled to expect. A

mujahid fights to uphold the cause of righteousness and for the supremacy of Islam; if in this fight he gets a share in the spoils of war, it is an extra favour to him. See also *khumus*.

'anwah fai' (عنوة فىء)
See *sulh fai*.

al-'aqār (العقار)
Lit: Immovable property. *Tech*: Relating to the law of *kharaj* and *ushr*, it includes immovable property and all other allied forms of property such as minerals, treasure trove and fruits on trees, etc.

al-'aqd (العقد)
Legal contract implying an enforceable act involving a bilateral declaration, namely, the offer (*ijab*) and the acceptance (*qabul*).

al-'āqid (العاقد)
Lit: One who contracts. *Tech*: In the law of *inan* partnership, the partner who enters into a transaction with a third party. The other partners are known as *muwakkil*. The jurisdiction of *al-aqid* has been defined specifically for different types of transactions. The *aqid* acts as the agent (*wakil*) of the remaining partners but not as surety (*kafil*) for them.

al-'āqilah (العاقله)
Lit: That group of people who share the blood-money liability of any one among them.

al-'aqrab fal 'aqrab (الأقرب فالأقرب)
An important juridical principle for distributing the wealth of a deceased. It means that the nearer ones of the deceased have a prior right over his wealth than the distant relations.

Arab Common Market (ACM)
Egypt, Iraq, Jordan and Syria formed the Arab Common Market in 1964 and abolished all tariffs on locally produced agricultural, animal and mineral products in 1971 and on

manufactured goods in 1973. Libya joined the ACM in 1977, Mauritania in 1980, PDR Yemen in 1982. These countries did not implement the free trade provisions until the end of 1985. In practice, non-tariff barriers were not removed.

al-ʿarāyā (العرايا)
See *bai al-araya*

al-ʾarḍ al-ʿādīyy (الأرض العادى)
Abandoned or dead lands without any traceable owners. See *al-ard al-mawat*.

ʾarḍ al-ʿafw (أرض العفو)
A category of *sulh* lands, the owners of which have left it and which Muslims have taken without fighting.

ʾarḍ al-ʿanwah (أرض العنوة)
Land conquered by force of arms without any agreement.

al-ʾarḍ al-baiḍāʾ (الأرض البيضاء)
Bare or uncultivated land, especially land without fruit trees.

ʾarḍ bil-bait al-māl (أرض بالبيت المال)
See *al-ard al-mamlakah*.

ʾarḍ al-baʿl (أرض البعل)
According to some, it consists of areas where the level of underground water stands so high that it brings moisture to deeply sunk plant roots, while others think it is the land that is watered by a sufficient supply of rainfall. Historically, these lands were also treated as ones which did not involve human labour for irrigation. Therefore, the taxation on them was the heaviest.

al-ʾarḍ ghair al-mamlūkah (الأرض غير المملوكة)
See *al-ard al-mubahah*.

ʾard al-ghīl. (أرض الغيل)
Lands irrigated by water dammed up in reservoirs or from

underground canals. Taxation of them was *ushr* or half-*ushr*, depending upon the investment involved in irrigation.

'arḍ al-ḥawz (أرض الحوز)
Land, the owner of which died without leaving an heir, which reverts to *bait al-mal*. It also applies as a general term to the land annexed to the *bait al-mal* by way of *ghanimah*.

al-'arḍ al-khāliṣah (الأرض الخالصة)
Those lands which have been declared as public property.

'arḍ al-kharāj (أرض الخراج)
Those lands which are owned by non-Muslims but have been conquered by Muslims either by force or by truce and have been left with the previous owners by the Islamic state. A land tax agreed to in the treaty or fixed by the state is levied on such lands.

'arḍ al-mamlakah (أرض المملكة)
The class of conquered lands whereby the rights of ownership have been vested in the state. In case of such lands, the cultivator is a state tenant and does not possess right of alienation or transfer. It is also known as *al-ard al hawz, al-ard al-sultaniyah* or *al-ard li-bait al mal*. Main sources of this type of land are (a) conquest of foreign lands not occupied by anyone at the time of conquest; (b) state accession of lands left by the heirless; (c) *khumus* of the conquered lands if distributed among soldiers; (d) lands conquered by storm and appropriated by the head of the state to the *bait al-mal*. These types of land are meant for the benefit of those who have the right to receive benefit from the *bait al-mal*.

al-arḍ al-mawāt (الأرض الموات)
Those lands located away from habitation whose owners are not traceable or were never occupied by anybody. Such land becomes the property of the person who develops and tills it. *Al-Mawat* do not include (a) those lands which serve a commu-

nity, such as meadows, woods for fuel, etc.; (b) those lands which are known to have such deposits of minerals as salt, coal-tar and petroleum and are required for the people at large; (c) those lands declared as state pastures (*hima*). According to some of the jurists, in order to avoid disputes possession of such lands must be preceded by permission from the state.

al-ʾarḍ al-mayyītah (الأرض الميتة)
'Dead' or abandoned lands whose owners are not traceable. See *al-ard al-mawat*.

al-ʾarḍ al-mubāḥah (الأرض المباحة)
Lands not owned or occupied by any identifiable person. Also known as *al-ard ghair al-mamlukah*. They are of three types: (a) those lands which provide common convenience to the inhabitants, such as streets, roads, drains, graveyards, mosques, grazing fields, etc., which cannot be owned by any particular person and even the state cannot impose proprietary restrictions on their use, known as *al-ard fana li baladah*; (b) those lands, consisting of jungles, barren fields, mountains, etc., which do not provide any common convenience, are not arable and are not owned by any one, also known as *al-mawat*; (c) those arable lands not owned by anyone, also known as *al-ard li-bait al-mal*.

al-ʾarḍ al-mukhtaṣṣah (الأرض المختصة)
The most fertile lands of fourteenth century A.D. Spain procured by the sultan. The agricultural proceeds were the property of the ruler.

ʾarḍ al-quniy (أرض القنى)
Land watered from underground canals. Tax on this land was lower than *ushr*, since they involved investment in irrigation.

ʾarḍ al-saiḥ (أرض السيح)
Lit: Lands irrigated by running water (of rivers and valleys). *Tech*: A category of land taxed most heavily since it involved the least human effort.

'arḍ al sail (أرض السيل)
Lit: Lands irrigated by rain-flooding. *Tech*: A category of land, taxed most heavily (like *ard al-saih*) because it involves the least human effort for irrigation.

al-'arḍ al-ṣulḥ (الأرض الصلح)
Lands of a conquered country for which there exists a provision in the agreement of the truce.

al-'arḍ al-sulṭānīyah (الأرض السلطانيه)
See *al-ard al-mamlakah*.

'arḍ al-timār (أرض التيمار)
A piece of land donated by the state to a person from out of heirless lands accessed to the *bait al-mal*. The donee gets the right to the produce of the land after paying for the subsistence of the tillers of the land. The ownership remains with the *bait al-mal*.

al-'arḍ al-'ushrīyah (الأرض العشرية)
It refers to all land owned by Muslims who pay *ushr* on it; the land, the owners of which accept Islam; the land of Arabia; and the land of those areas which were conquered by fighting and the land distributed among soldiers of the Muslim army.

'arḍ al-waqf (أرض الوقف)
The land which Muslims assign to the welfare of the community. See also *hima*.

al-'arīf (العريف)
Lit: Aware, cognizant, expert. *Tech*: The person who informs about *zakat* beneficiaries. He is included in the category of *amilin*.

al-'ārīyah (العارية)
Lit: Borrowed. *Tech*: To authorize someone to receive benefit from one's property without any consideration. It is one of the customs of Muslim society. People borrow quite frequently

small articles of household goods from neighbours and relatives, which is considered as a custom to promote love and co-operation among citizens (Quran 107:7). The difference between *ariyah* and *qard* is that in the former case, the thing borrowed (which is always other than money) is to be returned in its original form, whereas in the case of *qard*, the loan can be, and is usually, returned in money of equivalent value.

al-ʿārīyah al-maḍmūnah (العارية المضمونة)
A loan supported by a surety, guarantee or warranty.

al-ʾarzāq (الأرزاق)
Daily ration of wheat, barley and other foodgrains (including cloth) periodically distributed free among the people in the early days of Islam.

al-ʿaṣabah (العصبة)
Relating to the law of inheritance, those relatives in whose line of relationship no female enters. There is no fixed share of the *asabah* prescribed in the Quran. If the deceased is not survived by any *dhawul-faraid*, the whole of the property falls to the *asabah*, otherwise the residue of the *dhawul-faraid*. The *asabat* are the following relatives: (a) sons and daughters (grandsons/daughters in the absence of sons and daughters); (b) father, grandfather and great-grand-father, if there is no son, grandson, daughters and grand daughters); (c) in the absence of son, grandson, daughter, grand-daughter, father, grand-father, brother is an *asabah* including sons and daughters of the brother if the brother is not alive; (d) consanguine brother; if none of the above is alive; (e) full paternal uncle, if there is no consanguine brother.

ʾaṣḥāb al-maṭālib (أصحاب المطالب)
An institution of eighth century A.D., Egypt. Guilds which worked in close collaboration with the official mint (*dar al-sikkah*) to uncover hoarded wealth of tombs and funeraries. One-fifth of such discoveries was credited to the *bait al-mal* as *khumus*. The

hoarded gold from the tombs of Pharaohs was largely brought to circulation by the efforts of such guilds.

al-'āshir (العاشر)
Collectors of custom duties and *zakat* stationed by the state on the public roads.

al-'aṣl (الأصل)
See *al-diwan*.

al-'aṭā' (العطاء)
Annual pensions distributed among the people from out of *bait al-mal* during the early days of Islam.

al-'athariyy (العثرى)
Relating to the law of *ushr*, land irrigated by rainfall exclusively.

al-'awāmil (العوامل)
Relating to the law of *zakat*, animals employed for work or for tilling of land.

'ayāt al-fai' (آيات الفىء)
Verses 59:6–10 of the Quran relating to *fai*.

'ayāt al-kayy (آيات الكى)
Verses 9:34–35 of the Quran condemning accumulation of wealth.

'ayāt al-kanz (آيات الكنز)
Verses 9:34–35 of the Quran condemning accumulation of wealth.

B

Bahrain Islamic Bank (BIB)
Incorporated on 7 March 1979, operations began on 22 November 1979. Authorized capital, BD23 million. Subscribed capital, BD11.5 million, and paid-up capital, BD5.75 million.

al-bai' (البيع)
Lit: A contract of sale. *Tech*: Sale of definite goods or property with the free consent of parties for a definite price. It involves proposal (*ijab*) and acceptance (*qabul*). It has many types.

bai' 'ājlin bi-'ājilin (بيع آجل بعاجل)
Lit: Sale of something to be delivered later for a price to be paid immediately. *Tech*: It is an alternate term for *bai al-salam*.

bai' 'ājilin bi-'ājilin (بيع عاجل بآجل)
Lit: Sale of something to be delivered immediately for a price to be paid later. *Tech*: This is an alternate term for *bai al-muajjal*.

bai' al-'arīyyah (بيع العريه)
A sale in which some trees in the garden are donated by the owner to the poor who can get fresh fruit off these trees in exchange for the dry ones for household consumption and not for further sale. It is also known as *bai al-araya*.

bai' al-'aṣnām (بيع الأصنام)
Sale of idols, including the earnings of a sculptor.

bai' 'ala al-bai' (بيع على البيع)
Lit: Sale over the sale of another person. *Tech*: Attempts of a third person to sell his produce while the sale deal is in the process of being concluded between two persons. The intention of the third person is to upset the bargain. This is done usually by quoting a lower rate or pointing out defects in the goods being sold by the other seller.

bai 'atān fi bai 'ah (بيعتان فى بيعة)
A contract of sale in which a seller offers to sell for a certain price on cash but for a higher price on credit. It also applies to a situation in which a person sells merchandise for a certain price cash on the condition that the buyer will sell it back to him at a higher price on credit. Thus the first seller borrows a certain amount of money to be paid back with an increment (*riba*) sometime after. It is one of the contrivances to legitimize *riba*.

baiʿ bil barnāmaj (بيع بالبرنامج)

Sale of whole bales of goods on the basis of their description in an accompanying catalogue or list of contents (*barnamaj*) without actually unfolding the goods. This was in vogue in Medina and other Islamic cities in the first century A.H. and was treated as permissible by the *fuqaha*; otherwise wholesale trade would have been impossible.

al-baiʿ al-bāṭil (البيع الباطل)

An agreement of sale which is unlawful in respect of its substance and description. For example, an agreement of sale concluded by a lunatic or a minor is *batil* since it does not possess the substance of the agreement which is the proposal and acceptance by a sane or major person. Similarly, an agreement to sell a dead body or alcohol is not lawful since it involves exchange of *mal* for something valueless (*ghair mutaqawwam*).

baiʿ al-dain bil dain (بيع الدين بالدين)

Lit: Sale of a debt for a debt. *Tech*: A person agrees to sell a commodity to be delivered later for a price which he already owes to the intending buyer. Thus both the price as well as the product are in the form of debts.

baiʿ ḍarbah al-ghāʾiṣ (بيع ضربة الغائص)

A sales contract in which the buyer agrees to buy for a certain price whatever a diver will bring out from the bottom of river or ocean.

baiʿ ḍirāb al-jamal (بيع ضرب الجمل)

Hiring of a camel to cover a she-camel.

al-baiʿ al-fāsid (البيع الفاسد)

An agreement of sale which is lawful in its substance but unlawful in respect of its description. The substance of the agreement refers to proposal, acceptance and the article of sale. The description refers to characteristics other than the substance, such as the price of the article of sale. If an agreement of sale for a definite article is concluded by proposal and acceptance but the price is not settled, the agreement would be *fasid* although it is enforceable (*munaqad*) so far as its substance is concerned.

baiʿ al-fuḍūlī (بيع الفضولى)
An agreement of sale concluded by someone on the property of another without the permission of the latter.

baiʿ al-gharar (بيع الغرر)
Lit: A sale involving a risk. Aleatory sale. *Tech*: It is to sell a thing which one does not have in one's possession nor one expects to bring it under one's control, such as fish in the river or birds in the air. Possession is one of the basic conditions for a valid contract of sale. One cannot sell a thing which is not in one's possession; it involves risk for the buyer. *Bai al-gharar* is also a general term for all such sale deals which do not specify the commodity of sale or price or time of sale or where the ability of the seller to deliver the commodity is absent.

baiʿ ḥabal al-ḥabala (بيع حبل الحبلى)
A type of business transaction prevalent in pre-Islamic Arabia where the unborn child of a camel was sold while it was still in the womb.

baiʿ al-ḥāḍir li-bād (بيع حاضر لباد)
Lit: Sale by the urbanite for the nomadic. *Tech*: A type of business practice in the days of the Prophet whereby some people worked as agents of the grain-sellers from rural areas and all grain was sold through these agents. These agents earned profit both from the seller and the buyer and often deprived the cultivator of his just profit and the buyer of a just price.

baiʿ al-ḥaṣah (بيع الحصاة)
A type of business transaction in pre-Islamic Arabia where the contract was concluded by the buyer throwing pebbles towards the merchandise, the one hit by the pebble becoming the object sold.

bai‘ bi ’ilqā’ al-ḥajar (بيع بإلقاء الحجر)
An alternate term for *bai al-hasah*.

bai‘ al-‘īnah (بيع العينة)
A contract of sale where a person sells an article on credit and then buys back at a lesser price for cash. Example: A asks a loan of $10 from B. B, instead of asking for interest on this loan applies a contrivance. He sells an article to A for $12 on credit and then buys back from him the same article for cash at $10.

bai‘ ’istighlāl (بيع الإستغلال)
An alternate term for *bai bil wafa*.

bai‘ al-’istijrār (بيع الإستجرار)
A sales contract in which a person agrees to pay in lump sum in advance and receives the commodities gradually in instalments.

bai‘ al-’ist’imān (بيع الإستئمان)
A contract of sale in which the sale price is settled by accepting unquestionably the statement of the seller (regarding cost, etc.).

bai‘ al-’istiṣnā‘ (بيع الإستصناع)
A contract of sale in which a supplier (craftsman or manufacturer) is asked to supply goods of definite specifications at agreed rates, place and time of delivery.

bai‘ al-kālī’ bil kāli’ (بيع الكالىء بالكالىء)
Lit: A postponement or delay in the payment of a debt. *Tech*: A type of credit sales in which on the date of the discharge of the debt the debtor seeks extension with the promise to pay something in addition. In fact the amount of debt is sold to the debtor for some profit. What is meant by this is, a man's buying a thing on credit for a certain period and when the period of payment comes and he does not find anything to pay, he says to the creditor: sell it to me on credit for a further period for something additional. On this the creditor sells it to him. It may also refer to a man who pays money for wheat or the like, to be given at a

certain time and when the time comes the debtor says, 'I do not have wheat, etc., but you sell your debt to me on credit for a certain period with an increment'.

baiʿ al-khamr (بيع الخمر)
Sale of alcoholic drinks. It includes the preparation, filteration, carriage, storage and all allied activities, including the sale of containers and utensils of alcoholic drinks.

baiʿ al-khiyār (بيع الخيار)
Conditional sale. A sales contract which provides an option to the buyer to annul it. See *al-khiyar*.

baiʿ al-māʾ (بيع الماء)
Lit: Sale of water. *Tech*: Sale of surplus water of a natural source such as river, spring, canal, etc.

al-baiʿ al-mabrūr (البيع المبرور)
A sales contract which has no concealment of facts, dishonesty or doubt.

baiʿ al-maḍāmīn (بيع المضامين)
Lit: Sale of the contents. *Tech*: A sales contract in which a package is sold without specifying the contents.

baiʿ al-malāqīḥ (بيع الملاقيح)
Sale of the embryo or sale of what is in the womb of the female.

al-baiʿ al-mawqūf (البيع الموقوف)
An agreement of sale which is lawful in substance and description but is concluded with the consent of a third party who does not have an absolute right of ownership over the property of the buyer or the seller. For example, *bai al-fuduli*.

al-baiʿ al-muʾajjal (البيع المؤجل)
Lit: A credit sale. *Tech*: A financing technique adopted by Islamic banks. It is a contract in which the seller allows the buyer

to pay the price of a commodity at a future date in a lump sum or in instalments. The price fixed for the commodity in such a transaction can be the same as the spot price or higher or lower than the spot price.

baiʿ al-muʿāṭah (بيع المعاطاة)
See *bai al-ta ati*.

baiʿ al-muḍṭar (بيع المضطر)
To purchase a thing when its owner is compelled under stress of want to dispose of it.

baiʿ al-muḥaqlah (بيع المحاقلة)
A type of business transaction whereby grains in ears are sold for dry grain.

baiʿ al-mukhāṭarah (بيع المخاطرة)
An alternate term for *bai al-gharar*.

baiʿ al-mulāmasah (بيع الملامسة)
A form of sales contract prevalent in the days of the Prophet in which the buyer or the seller used to touch a piece of cloth and this very act of touching finalized the sales deal.

baiʿ al-munābadhah (بيع المنابذة)
A contract of sale prevalent in the days of the Prophet in which the seller or the buyer would throw a piece of cloth towards the other and this very act of throwing finalized the sales deal.

al-baiʿ al-munʿaqad (البيع المنعقد)
Lit: An enforceable contract of sale. *Tech*: A contract to exchange *mal* when one party proposes and the other accepts it. It can be of four types: *sahih, fasid, nafidh* or *mawquf*.

baiʿ al-muqayaḍah (بيع المقايضة)
Selling a commodity for another commodity. Barter exchange.

baiʿ al-murābaḥah (بيع المرابحة)
Lit: Sale on profit. *Tech*: A contract of sale in which the seller declares his cost and profit. This has been adopted (with certain modifications) as a mode of financing by a number of Islamic banks. As a financing technique, it involves a request by the client to the bank to purchase a certain item for him. The bank does that for a definite profit over the cost which is settled in advance. Many people have questioned the legality of this financing technique because of its great similarity with *riba*.

baiʿ al-musāwamah (بيع المساومة)
Lit: Haggling, bargaining. *Tech*: Sale of goods at a price on which the buyer and seller agree after haggling without mentioning the cost of the seller.

baiʿ al-muzābanah (بيع المزابنة)
It is the exchange of fresh fruits for dry ones in a way that the quantity of the dry fruit is actually measured and fixed but the quantity of the fresh fruit to be given in exchange is guessed while it is still on trees.

baiʿ al-muzāyadah (بيع المزايدة)
Lit: A public sale through auction in which the deal is struck with the highest bidder. *Tech*: A form of sale of a merchandise in which more than one seller is interested, and before the deal is finalized some of the prospective customers start bidding up the price without the intention of buying it.

al-baiʿ al-nāfidh (البيع النافذ)
A contract of sale which does not involve any right of the third party. It is of two types: *lazim* (binding) and *ghair lazim* (non-binding). The *lazim* is a contract of sale which has no options (to rescind) for any of the parties and the *ghair lazim* is a contract of sale which may have at least one option for any of the parties.

baiʿ al-najash (بيع النجش)
See *al-tanajush*.

bai' bil nasī'ah (بيع بالنسيئة)
Credit sale with a fixed term to pay up the agreed price. This method of *bai bil nasiah* usually resulted in *riba* dealings in the pre-Islamic days and caused multiplication of the original price if not paid back at the stipulated time.

al-bai' al-qaṭ'ī (البيع القطعى)
A contract of sale which is final and binding in all respects.

al-bai' bil raqm (البيع بالرقم)
A sales contract prevalent in pre-Islamic Arabia in which the merchandise was sold with reference to certain mark or sign on it without the buyer knowing its exact quantity.

al-bai' al-ṣaḥīḥ (البيع الصحيح)
A contract of sale which is lawful in its substance and description. The substance of an agreement refers to *proposal, acceptance* and the *article* of sale (*mabi*).

bai' al-salam (بيع السلم)
It is defined as advance payment for goods which are to be delivered later. According to normal rules no sale can be affected unless the goods are in existence at the time of the bargain, but this sort of sale forms an exception to the general rule provided the goods are defined and the date of delivery is fixed. The objects of this sale are mostly fungible things and cannot be gold or silver because they are regarded as monetary values. Barring this, *bai al-salam* covers almost all things which are capable of being definitely described as to quantity, quality and workmanship. One of the conditions of this contract is advance payment; the parties cannot reserve their option of rescinding it but the option of revoking it on account of a defect in the subject matter is allowed. It is also applied to a mode of financing adopted by Islamic banks. It is usually applied in the agricultural sector where the bank advances money for various inputs to receive a share in the crop (which the bank sells in the market).

baiʿ al-ṣarf (بيع الصرف)
Sale of monetary value for monetary value.

baiʿ-as-ṣikāk (بيع الصكاك)
Lit: Sale through documents. *Tech*: To buy certain goods without taking possession except through transferring of papers of entitlement. This was common in the early days of Islam and is also prevalent in the modern times in futures markets. Sale deals are concluded without physical possession of goods from one party to the other, from second to third and third to fourth, and so on. At each stage margins are added without adding any utility to the products. They are all covered under *bai al-sikak*. Similarly, selling only licences and permits issued by the government is also covered by this.

baiʿ al-ṣubrah (بيع الصبرة)
A form of sales contract in which a heap of foodgrains (or any other commodity) is sold without measuring or weighing.

al-baiʿ al-ṣūrī (البيع الصورى)
An alternate term for *bai al-taljiah*.

al-baiʿ bil tākhīr (البيع بالتآخير)
A contract of sale in which the payment has been deferred.

baiʿ al-talji'ah (بيع التلجئة)
Lit: A sales contract which is contrary to what it appears. *Tech*: It is a simulated sale in which the seller pretends to have sold his property when in fact he has not. For example, a person may show that he has sold his property to his son so that the state may not confiscate it. In recent times this phenomenon was observed when in certain Muslim states the feudal lords transferred their lands to their relatives to avoid confiscation under land reforms regulations. It also refers to delaying tactics of a defaulting debtor in which he transfers his property or assets apparently to a third party for fear of creditors claiming a right on those assets against their debts. In fact the assets are not transferred to

anyone but it is posed as if they have been transferred. The third party whose name is used is also made to testify such a transfer though the claim is untrue.

baiʿ al-taʿāṭī (بيع التعاطى)
A sales contract whereby the buyer picks up the goods and the seller accepts the price without any explicit bargain. It is also termed as *bai al muatah*.

baiʿ al-tawlīyah (بيع التولية)
A contract of sale in which the seller agrees to sell a product at his cost.

baiʿ al-ʿurbān (بيع العربان)
It is getting a thing against a nominal advance on the condition that if the bargain is struck, the advance will be adjusted and if the bargain is cancelled, the seller will not return the advance. The advance being nominal, the buyer had practically no liability. He will abide by the contract if he finds it advantageous to him and will withdraw from it otherwise. The modern day options contracts in the stock exchange are covered by *bai al-urban*.

baiʿ al-waḍīʿah (بيع الوضيعة)
A sales contract in which a seller informs the buyer his actual cost and then gives a further discount on it. Thus it is a sale at a loss.

baiʿ bil-wafāʾ (بيع بالوفا)
A sales agreement in which the buyer agrees to return the goods at the same price once the agreement is concluded. It is permissible if the clause for returning the goods is not instituted before-hand. But if the said clause is the essence of the contract the agreement becomes void.

bait al-māl (بيت المال)
Lit: Public treasury. *Tech*: An institution of early and mediaeval Islam, it functioned as the central bank of the state, state insurance company and controller of domestic and foreign trade. The

bait al-mal had two main categories: *bait al mal al-ammah*, the ordinary revenues of the state and *bait al mal al-khassah*, revenues accruing to the ruler from crown domains (*diya al-khassah*). The *khalifah* or his *wazir* would re-appropriate funds from one category of the *bait al-mal* to the other. The *diwan bait al-mal* kept the accounts and was subject to audit by *diwan al-zimam*. The head of *bait al mal* was known as *sahib bait al-mal*. The *sahib* had the right to inspect *diwan al-kharaj*. Besides central *bait al-mal*, there were *buyut al-amwal* at the provinces. The *khazin* connected to these *buyut al-amwal* was responsible for taxes paid in kind and stored at other financial centres.

bait al-māl al-ʿāmmah (بيت المال العامه)
See *bait al-mal*.

bait al-māl al-khāṣṣah (بيت المال الخاصة)
Private treasury of the caliph to cover his personal, family and executive expenditure. It seems that the *bait al-mal al-khassah* did not appear until the caliphate of Muawiyah had become more distinct under the Ottoman empire.

bait māl al-muslimīn (بيت المال المسلمين)
Public treasury of the Muslims for collecting and disbursing charity and *waqf* funds. Usually, it was administered by the chief *qadi* of the state. The funds were kept in the mosque under safe custody. The chief *qadi* was responsible to administer these funds strictly in accordance with the *shariah*.

al-bakhs (البخس)
Lit: Too little, too low, very low (price). *Tech*: Quranic term for exploitative decrement in value to others by traders in contracts of sale. The people of Madyan during the life-time of Prophet Shuaib used to exploit the strangers by colluding with each other and declaring genuine money (coins) of the strangers as false or spurious. The stranger would, thus, sell those coins to them at a low price. Thus they would deprive the ignorant stranger by collusion and deceit.

al-baꜥl (البعل)

Relating to the law of *ushr*, trees which fetch their moisture from land (without any rainfall). *Ushr* is levied on the produce of these trees. See *ard al-bal*.

al-baqarah al-muthīrah (البقرة المثيرة)

Relating to the law of *zakat*, a cow or bull engaged in tilling of land.

al-Baraka Islamic Investment Bank Bahrain (AIIB)

Incorporated on 21 February 1984. Authorized capital, US$2 million. Paid-up capital, US$ .50 million.

al-barakāh (البركة)

Lit: Blessings. *Tech*: God's blessing or bounty in relation to one's worldly pursuits. It refers to qualitative growth in one's possessions.

al-Barakah International Limited

al-Barakah International is a licensed deposit taker and the first Islamic Bank in Britain within the framework of the Banking Act of the country.

al-barīd (البريد)

Tech: A measure of distance equivalent to 4 *farasikh*, 4,800 *dhira* or 22.176 kilometres. Also used for the beast of burden which carries the mail and for the postman who used to ride that animal.

al-bāṭil (الباطل)

Lit: Futile, false, vain, invalid, void. *Tech*: A juristic expression about something which is unlawful in its substance as well as its description (*wasf*). The Hanafite jurists distinguish between *batil* and *fasid*, the latter denoting something which is not inherently void but has conditions or characteristics which has made it void. Other jurists do not distinguish between *batil* and *fasid*.

al-bāzil (البازل)
Relating to the *nisab* for *zakat*, a camel that has reached eight years old and entered into the ninth year.

al-biḍā'ah (البضاعة)
A form of quasi-agency in mediaeval trading. It involved a merchant who, unable personally to attend to a business affair, hands over some of his property to another party for the latter to take care of it for him. Upon completion of his task the outside party, without receiving any commission, profit or compensation in any other form returns the proceeds of the transaction to the merchant whose bidding he has done. All parties to a partnership or *mudarabah* contract are endowed with the right to exercise this practice freely because it is one of the accompaniments of trade. It is often practised on reciprocal basis by the merchants for each other.

BIMB
Bank Islam Malaysia Berhard, established on 1 July 1983. First Islamic Bank of Malaysia.

bint labūn (بنت لبون)
Relating to the *nisab* for *zakat*, a she camel in her third year.

bint makhāḍ (بنت مخاض)
Relating to the *nisab* for *zakat*, a she-camel in her second year.

al-birr (البر)
Lit: Reverence, piety, kindness, charitable gift. *Tech*: To adopt a generous attitude in interpersonal and inter-institutional dealings. See also *al-ihsan*.

borrowing ratio
Used in the model of interest-free banking based on *mudarabah*, it is the ratio of the interest-free loans given by the central bank to the member banks and interest-free loans of the member banks to the public.

BRP
Bankers Ratio of Profit-sharing. Percentage share of the bank in the entrepreneur's profits on finance taken on the basis of *mudarabah*. It is an Islamic alternative to the interest on credit obtained by entrepreneurs.

buy-back
A mode of financing adopted by banks in Pakistan. According to this agreement the bank purchases moveable or immovable property for the client with the agreement that the client would buy it back from the bank at a higher price, to be paid later by the client.

C

Cairo Geniza
See *Geniza*.

central deposits (CD)
One of the proposed monetary policy tools for a *riba*-free economy. The central bank may open investment accounts in its member banks in which it deposits whatever money it creates and from which it withdraws whatever money it retires. Member banks may invest these deposits in the real sector in accordance with the investment policy of each bank. Profits earned on such deposits may be used to cover the cost of central bank operations. Such deposits, termed as CDs or central deposits, may be used both as a tool of monetary policy and a means of financial intermediation. The central bank may create an instrument which could be termed as 'central deposit certificate' or CDC. The CDCs may be invested in CDs throughout the banking system. The rate of return on the CDCs will approach the average rate of profit on investment for the whole economy. The central bank may keep CDs in foreign exchange with members banks, should it have a surplus of foreign

exchange. The central bank may issue CDCs denominated in foreign currencies. The proceeds of foreign exchange thus collected may be invested through member banks. These may be utilized to meet foreign exchange requirements. The central bank may use CDs to supply domestic currency in return for foreign exchange earnings of the residents. This would keep the nominal supply of money from increasing beyond the desired level.

central deposit certificates (CDC)
An instrument of *riba*-free banking. The certificate would be offered by the central bank to the general public and would denominate deposits with the central bank. The central bank will invest these with all member banks, which makes it the most diversified investment in the economy. Since it involves two layers of financial intermediation, namely, member banks and the central bank, it would be the safest instrument available.

central lending certificates (CLC)
One of the proposed monetary policy tools in *riba*-free economy. The central bank may issue CLCs which carry no return, but are guaranteed to be paid on maturity. This would be a medium for the public to extend their funds as *qard hasan* with altruistic motives. Proceeds of CLCs may be made available to member banks which would lend them to borrowers after proper assessment of future income and application of social criteria if rationing is required.

COMCEC
The Standing Committee for Commercial and Economic Cooperation of the OIC. Founded in 1981 in Taif (Saudi Arabia) as an organ of the OIC, COMCEC works for the Summit Conference of the OIC, which is held every three years.

commenda
Lit: *Mudarabah*. The orientalists use the term commenda interchangeably with mudarabah.

commodity-Muḍārabah
A contract of *mudarabah* wherein the owner of capital provides the capital in the form of stock-in-trade (urud).

D

al-dain (الدين)
Lit: debt, liability. *Tech*: It is a liability created by a contract, expenditure or deḅt. *Al-dain* has a definite term fixed for repayment as distinguished from *al-qard*, which does not have a fixed term for maturity.

al-dain al-ḍaʿīf (الدين الضعيف)
A debt which has accrued without the exchange of any tangible asset. Unpaid wages of the worker, undistributed inheritance and provident funds deducted at source are some of the examples.

dain ghair marjū al-ʾadāʾ (دين غير مرجو الأداء)
See *dain marju al-ada*.

dain marjū al-ʾadāʾ (دين مرجوا الأداء)
Relating to the law of *zakat*, it refers to the debt expected to be returned by the debtor. In other words, it refers to debts assessed to be good as against bad debts (*dain ghair marju al-ada*). It is also known as *dain thabit*.

al-dain al-muʾajjal (الدين المؤجل)
Lit: Deferred debt. *Tech*: Debt in the pre-Islamic days, with the creditors' stipulation of an increase in the amount for increase in term of repayment. The deferred debt, added to which were the continuous increases over the subsequent terms, would double and re-double.

al-dain al mustaghriq (الدين المستغرق)
Claims against an estate which exceed or equal its value.

al-dain al-muṭlaq (الدين المطلق)

A debt not bound to the physical person of the debtor but outliving him.

al-dain al-qawī (الدين القوى)

A debt which has accrued as a result of exchange of a tangible asset such as a loan or trade.

al-dain al-thābit (الدين الثابت)

See *dain marju al-ada*.

al-dālīyah (الدالية)

Relating to the law of *zakat*, it refers to a small bucket tied to the cattle working on a well to irrigate land. Half *ushr* (5 per cent) is levied on lands irrigated by *al-daliyah*. It is also known as *al-naura*.

al-ḍamān (الضمان)

Lit: Responsibility, guarantee, warranty, surety. *Tech*: Surety against and responsibility for all insurable risks as well as uncertainty. The shariah has made the responsibility of the entrepreneur to cover all these risks since he is the one who receives the profit. There cannot accrue any lawful profit to someone who refuses to accept these risks.

ḍamān al-darak (ضمان الدرك)

Surety by the seller against any defect in the title of the property.

ḍamān 'alā khaṭar al-ṭarīq (ضمان على خطر الطريق)

An agreement whereby a person undertakes to indemnify another person if the latter suffers a loss during a journey, provided that the traveller undertakes the journey on the same route as identified by the indemnifier.

ḍamān al-khusrān (ضمان الخسران)

Lit: Surety for loss. *Tech*: Standing surety for someone's loss in a business. An application has been made of this principle in the case of *riba*-free banking. The state cannot hold out a guarantee to the depositors of a *riba*-free bank to make good any loss in the deposits through *mudarabah* or *shirkah* with the bank.

ḍamān al-naqṣ (ضمان النقص)
Liability for making-up any loss. It relates to contract for deposits or in *riba*-free banking. The *riba*-free bank is liable to make up any deficiency in the demand deposits of the creditors. The bank is also liable to make up the lossess, in case a loss occurs due to violation of the terms of a particular investment deposit. Both the situations are governed by the juridical concept of *daman al-naqs*.

ḍamān al-talaf (ضمان التلف)
Guarantee to make good any loss which may occur to the property of someone while in safe custody of the guarantor. The term has been applied in the model of *riba*-free banking where the bank guarantees demand deposits against any loss.

ḍamān al-ta'rrūḍ (ضمان التعرض)
Surety by the seller to the purchaser against any dispute about the property by a third party or by the seller himself.

al-dāniq (الدانق)
Lit: An ancient coin, a small coin. *Tech*: A coin of silver equal to eight grains of barley or 0.496 grams.

dār al-'ahd (دار العهد)
Lands over which there is a peace treaty between the Muslims and the non-Muslims.

dār al-ḥarb (دار الحرب)
The lands of non-Muslims who have declared war against Muslims.

dār al-Islām (دار الإسلام)
The land of Muslims where they live in peace and according to Islamic principles.

dār al-māl al-Islāmī (دار المال الاسلامی)
A holding company, registered in the Bahamas with a paid-up capital of US$1,000 million contributed by the promoters and the public in Muslim countries. The affairs of the DMI are conducted under the direction of an eighteen-member board of supervisors. Administration of the business affairs of the DMI is entrusted to Dar al-Mal al-Islami, S.A. (DMISA), a corporation formed under the laws of the Canton of Geneva, Switzerland. All the shares of the DMISA are owned by the DMI. The DMI operates through Islamic banks, investment and insurance companies. The DMI invests in banking companies as well, provided that it is allowed to hold 51 per cent of the equity. The DMI claims to run its affairs on an interest-free basis. A board of shariah scholars supervises the legality of the DMI's business in the eyes of the shariah. The investment companies of the DMI accept deposits on various terms. The DMI acts as a *mudarib* and the depositors are treated as *arbab al-amwal*. The insurance companies of the DMI, known as *takaful* or solidarity companies cover known losses. The membership of these companies brings all the members into a union of brotherhood where the loss of one is made up by others. The premiums received are invested in lawful business. Any profits are also distributed among all the members, DMI keeping a small commission for its services.

dār al-ṭirāz (دار الطراز)
Royal textile factories of mediaeval Islamic era.

al-ḍarā'ib (sing. daribah) (الضرائب)
Levies imposed by an Islamic state on its citizens at times of such emergencies as natural calamities, famine, war, etc. These taxes were levied only when normal sources of revenue were inadequate to meet the immediate expenses.

al-ḍarb fil'arḍ (الضرب فی الارض)
Quranic term for struggle to earn one's livelihood. By implication it is applied to struggle for *halal rizq*.

ḍarībah al ṭaʿām (ضريبة الطعام)
Kharaj of land assessed and paid in kind. The term was prevalent in Egypt during the early period of Islam.

al-ḍarūrīyāt al-khams (الضروريات الخمس)
Lit: The five fundamental needs. *Tech*: Five basic needs of every Muslim, namely, protection of life, religion (*din*), reason (*aql*), progeny and property. They have also been termed as *maqasid al-shariah*, i.e., the main objectives of the shariah. An Islamic state is supposed to cater for these basic needs of all its inhabitants, should the individual, the family or his community be unable to do it.

dhawu al-ʾarḥām, (ذو الأرحام)
Relating to the law of inheritance, relations connected through females. They get a share in the absence of *dhaw-u l-faraid* and *asabat*. The following relatives come under this category:

a. Son of the daughter and daughter of the daughter.
b. Son of the daughter of the son, and daughter of the daughter of the son and their children.
c. Maternal grandfather, maternal grandfather of the father, the grandfather of the mother, maternal grandfather of the mother, the grandmother of the mother, children of the sisters, sisters of the father and those of the mother, etc.

dhawu al-farāʾiḍ (ذو الفرائض)
Relating to the law of inheritance. These are the people whose shares have been defined in the Quran. They are twelve in number; (a) four males: father, grandfather, uterine brothers and husband; (b) eight females: wife, daughters, son's daughter, mother, grandmother, full sister, consanguine sister, uterine sister.

dhimmah lands
Lands in possession of *dhimmis* in exchange for land taxes. Also known as *ard al-kharaj*.

al-dhimmi (الذمى)

Non-Muslims who came under the protection of the Islamic state after fighting and accepting the defeat. They are to be distinguished from *al-muahid* (contractees) who agreed to live under Muslim protection as a result of some peace agreement. *Al-Muahids* are liable to pay tax according to the agreement whereas *al-dhimmis* are subject to *jizyah*.

al-dhirāʿ (الذراع)

Lit: arm, forearm, cubit. *Tech*: measures of different length prevalent in the mediaeval era in Muslim countries.

dhirāʿ al-ʾāmmah (ذراع العامة)

Also known as *dhira al-kirbas*, a cubit equivalent to 46.2 cm.

dhirāʿ al-daur (ذراع الدور)

See *dhira al-qasabah*.

al-dhirāʿ al-hāshmiyyah (ذراع الهاشميه)

A cubit devised by Abu Musa al-Ashari prevalent in Kufa and Basra. One *dhira al-Hashmiyyah* was equal to 61.6 cm or 3.79456 metres.

al-dhirāʿ al-mirāthīyyah (ذراع المراثية)

A cubit devised by al-Mamun to measure *barid* (post stages), embankments, *suqs*, canals and excavations, equal to one *dhira al-Sawad* plus two-thirds of the same plus two-thirds of a finger.

dhirāʿ al-misāḥah (ذراع المساحة)

A cubit to measure land. One dhira al-misahah was equal to 106.68 cm.

dhirāʿ muqaddar al-sharʿī (ذراع مقدر الشرعى)

The legal cubit used in the shariah is 46.2 cm. It was also known as *dhira al-ammah*.

al-dhirāʿ al-qaṣabah (ذراع القصبة)
A cubit measuring two-thirds finger less than *dhira al-Sawad*. It was devised by Ibn Abi Laila (the qadi). One qasabah is 369.6 cm or 13.660416 sq. metres.

dhirāʿ al-Sawad (ذراع السواد)
The cubit of Sawad, devised by al-Rashid who determined it from the forearm of a negro slạve. It was used for cloth, merchandise, buildings and for the milometer.

al-dhirāʿ al-ʿUmarīyyah (ذراع العمرية)
A cubit devised by Umar b. al-Khattab to measure lands of *Sawad*. It measured a cubit (prevalent) plus a grip of clasped hand and a thumb.

al-dhirāʿ al-yusufīyya (ذراع اليوسفية)
A cubit measuring ⅔ finger less than *dhira al-Sawad*. It was devised by Imam Abu Yusuf to measure lands of Baghdad.

DIB
See Dubai Islamic Bank.

al-ḍimār (الضمار)
See māl al-dimar.

al-dinār (الدينار)
Lit: A monetary unit. *Tech*: Gold coin weighing one *mithqal*, equivalent to 4.25 grams.

al-dinār alʿainī
Copper *dinar* in circulation during *Nasrid* Spain (fourteenth century AD). It was used for day-to-day internal exchange and carried a fixed monetary value.

al-dinār al-dhahabī (الدينار الذهبى)
Golden *dinar* in circulation during *Nasrid* Spain. Usually of 2 grams in weight, containing 22 carats gold. The gold *dinar* was

mostly used in the international trade in those days. It was equal to 5 to 7 silver *dinars* or 75 silver *dirhams*.

al-dinār al-fiḍḍī (الدينار الفضى)
Silver *dinar* in circulation during *Nasrid* Spain, usually equal to 1/15th to 1/7th of a gold *dinar*. Silver *dinars* were of square shape and seem to have been issued by Nasri rulers with fixed monetary value as compared to gold *dinars*, which had a fluctuating market price.

dirham lil-ʾashyāʾ (درهم للأشياء)
Lit: A weight of varying magnitude. *Tech*: A weight to weigh commodities. One *dirham* equals 3.171 grams.

dirham al-fiḍḍah (درهم الفضه)
Lit: A weight of varying magnitude. *Tech*: Silver coin weighing one *dirham*. Equal to the weight of 70 grains of barley or 2.97675 grams.

al-dīwān (الديوان)
Lit: Account books of the treasury. *Tech*: The finance department of early Muslim states. Initially established by caliph Umar as a department to manage state finances, but later on adopted by Muslim states on a regular basis. The entire economic activity came to be co-ordinated through *diwan bait al-mal* being one of its wings. During the Abbaside period the *diwan* became a generic name for a department. Each department came to be designated as *diwan* relating to specific functions. Each *diwan* had two sections: *al-asl* (shortened from *majalis al asl* or *diwan al asl*) and *al-zimam*. The former was the main office while the latter was a supervising bureau (and was also called *diwan al-ishraf* because of that reason). The *asl* section was responsible for preparing the departmental budget and its execution while *al-zimam* was responsible for audit and control. In addition to a *zimam* section with each department, there was a *zimam* for public undertakings or state property.

dīwān al-ahshām (ديوان الأحشام)
See *diwan al-nafaqat*.

dīwān al-ʾazimmah (ديوان الأزمة)
A supreme audit office established by Abbasides to control and check the accounts of other *diwans*. This was also termed as *diwan zimam al-azimmah*.

dīwān bait al-māl (ديوان بيت المال)
See *bait al-mal*.

dīwān al-birr wa al-ṣadaqah (ديوان البر والصدقة)
A department during the Abbaside period responsible for distributing that part of *zakat* on which the poor, needy and the *awqaf* had a claim.

dīwān al-ḍaiyah (ديوان الضيعة)
Central board for the management of personal estates of the caliph during the Abbaside caliphate.

dīwān al-ḍiyāʿ (ديوان الضياع)
An office set up by early Abbasides to oversee estates, properties, investments and rents of the state. See also *diwan al-mal*.

dīwān duar al-ḍurūb (ديوان دور الضروب)
A department for controlling local mints. Originally started by Ummayyads, it grew into a modern day central bank. It kept an eye on the circulation of money and granted concession of coinage.

dīwān al-jahbadhah (ديوان الجهبذة)
See *jahbadh*.

dīwān al-kharāj (ديوان الخراج)
Finance department of the central government during the Abbaside period. It had a number of wings. *Majalis al-asl* (where the chief used to sit) was responsible for drawing financial esti-

mates. There was *majalis al-hisab* for reviewing the provincial accounts before they were ratified in the *majalis al-jamaah*, the bureau for closing the accounts of local *buyut al-amwal*. Then there were *majalis al-sudan*, probably a bureau for drafts or perhaps for keeping registers and *majalis al-tafsil* which kept specified charts over individual tax-payers, their circumstances, yields, and correspondence regarding their problems. Finally, it contained *majalis al-jaysh* that kept an eye on the military participation on tax levy and the *tasabbub* that flowed to them. *Diwan al-kharaj* functioned independently of other departments. It acted as an audit office over the wazirs, and also looked after the agricultural and economic productivity of the provinces.

dīwān al-khazā'in (ديوان الخزائن)
A department during the Abbaside period, responsible for governmental stores of natural products, magazines and arsenals.

dīwān al-mā' (ديوان الماء)
A department during the Abbaside period responsible for irrigation works. In case of private *diya* the owner was responsible for maintenance of irrigation works. This department also supervised distribution of irrigation water. The department kept accounts of the agricultural outputs and fed *diwan al-kharaj* with data for calculating *ibrah* (average output).

dīwān al-māl (ديوان المال)
Provincial department of revenue which kept registers defining each province and indicating how it had been annexed to the Muslim state, whether by *anwah* or *sulh*. Registration covered the status of land taxation at various points, indicating whether the payments were *kharaj* or *ushr*, whether *kharaj* was considered as rent or as a *jizyah*, the survey of the land with the names of holders, the type of *kharaj* assessment, whether it was *misah* or *muqasamah*, and the fixed rate of *kharaj* in the case of *misahah* or the proportion of yield in case of *muqasamah*. Moreover, sufficient information was kept about the mines and their payments or the *ushur* of trade. The payers of the *jizyah* were also listed.

dīwān al-maqbūḍāt (ديوان المقبوضات)
See *diwan al-musadarin*.

dīwān al-muṣādarīn (ديوان المصادرين)
A department during the Abbaside period which dealt with matters concerning those officials who were called to account for the way in which they discharged their duties and in consequence were penalized and sometimes deprived of their property. The methods employed at *musadarah* might range from a polite discussion in which the accused might voluntarily submit to pay a fine, to torture and even loss of life. The *diwan* was also responsible for the management of confiscated properties. Therefore, in certain cases it was also known as *diwan al-maqbudat*.

dīwān al-mustaghallāt (ديوان المستغلات)
An administrative office established by the Ummayyads to administer state lands, including government properties in cities and villages and their rents. It is likely, however, that this *diwan* was a small department attached to the larger and more important *diwan al kharaj*.

dīwān al-nafaqāt
An office established by early Abbasides to manage the expenditure of the state as they related to the requirements of the court. It dealt with the salaries of the court officials, provisions, construction and repair of royal buildings and care of stables. As many of the expenses in this department went to the retinue of the *khalifah*, it was also called *diwan al-ahsham*. It was divided into *majalis al-jari*, the place where the pay of the *ahsham* was disbursed, the *majalis al-inzal* from where the household of the *khalifah* was financed and where accounts were settled with the merchants, who paid in the *wazifah*, and where the natural products grown upon the governmental *diya* were delivered and controlled. It also had *majalis al hawadith* responsible for extraordinary expenses.

dīwān al-sawād (ديوان السواد)
An office set up by early Abbasides to act as agent for collection of all revenues and taxes from the agricultural lands of Iraq.

dīwān al-ṣawāfī (ديوان الصوافي)
Central board for the management of *sawafi* lands during the Abbaside period.

dīwān-i-wizārat (ديوان وزارت)
Relating to the administration of *iqta* in India of the sixteenth century. It was the central accounts office which was also the chief auditing authority of the revenue receipts of the provincial *iqta*.

al-ḍiyāʿ (الضياع)
Private estates either belonging to the crown or to private owners. In contradistinction to private estates, the crown estates were also called *diya al-sultan* or *diya al-khalifah*. These consisted of confiscated estates as well as such estates that had been purchased.

ḍiyāʿ al-khalīfah
See *al-diya*.

ḍiyāʿ al-khāṣṣah (ضياع الخاصة)
Also known as *diya al-mustakhlisah*, they were private estates belonging to the crown. The income from them accrued to the *bait al-mal al-khassah*.

ḍiyāʿ al-mustakhliṣah (ضياع المستخلصة)
See *diya al-khassah*.

ḍiyāʿ al-sulṭān (ضياع السلطان)
See *al-diya*.

DMI
See *Dar al-Mal al-Islami*.

DRP
Depositors' Rate of Profit-sharing. In interest-free banking, percentage share of depositors in the profits accruing to the banks. It is an Islamic alternative to interest on saving bank deposits.

double muḍārabah
An arrangement according to which capital is advanced to an intermediary (be it a bank, a finance corporation or business firm), on the basis of *mudarabah* which further gives this capital to a third party again on the basis of *mudarabah*. In this way two independent contracts take place. The intermediary (say I) enters into contract with the one who advances money on the basis of *mudarabah* (say S), and the one who takes it on the basis of *mudarabah* (say E). The profit from the business of E, shall be distributed between 'E' and 'I' in a given proportion, but any loss on the capital shall be borne by 'I' alone. Similarly, any profit earned by 'I' shall be shared by 'S' and 'I' in a pre-determined ratio but any loss to 'I' shall be borne by 'S' alone. In this way 'I' acts as agent, and E sub- agent of S.

Dubai Islamic Bank (DIB)
Incorporated on 10 March 1975. Has three branches in UAE. Authorized capital, 50 million dirhams (fully paid-up).

dukhūl fil-'arḍ (دخول فى الأرض)
Purchase or lease of *kharaj* land by a Muslim which was originally banned.

E

effective capital
Used in relation to *riba*-free financing by some writers, who profess that profit-loss sharing should not be proportionate to face-value of capital but should be pro-rata 'effective capital'. The sum of effective capital is to be a factor of exposure to risk

and period of investment. It would be arrived at by multiplying the face-value of capital by a 'risk exposure factor'. The share of profits of a particular class of capital to the total profits will bear the same ratio as the *effective capital* of that class bears to the *total effective capital*. See also *risk exposure factor*.

emanet
See *al-muqataah*.

F

al-faḍl (الفضل)
Lit: Surplus. *Tech*: Bounties of God. Used in connection with struggle to earn livelihood and attain bounties of God.

al-fai' (الفىء)
Lit: Return, booty, shadow. *Tech*: Signifies what is obtained from the enemies after laying down arms (without fighting) and what is received from any alien people under a treaty, the proceeds of which, according to the majority of jurists, go to the public sector of the Islamic state. According to some, however, a fifth of the *fai*, like that of *ghanimah*, is to be divided among the five categories specified for the latter: the Prophet, his near relatives, destitutes, orphans and poor way-farers. After the demise of the Prophet the two shares of the Prophet and his relatives from the fifth of the *fai* and *ghanimah* as held by the majority were withheld by Abu Bakr and this practice was followed by the subsequent three caliphs also. These two shares were either absorbed in the shares of the other three beneficiaries or as some reports say, went to the general public sector. Subsequently, the *fai* came to be identified with all revenues except *zakat*, a term which can mean civil revenues these days.

fai' al-muslim (فىء المسلم)
An alternate term for *fai*.

al-faij (الفيج)
Special messengers running with letters of credit, employed by bankers during the Abbaside period. This was a regular banking service provided for a small commission (usually one *dirham* per *dinar*).

Faisal Finance Institution Turkey (FFIT)
Incorporated on 9 October 1984. Authorized capital, TL5 billion (all paid-up).

Faisal Islamic Bank of Egypt (FIBE)
The Faisal Islamic Bank of Egypt was founded in 1977 by Prince Muhammad al-Faisal al-Saud. It claims to run its operations on the basis of the *shariah*. A board of *ulema* supervises the legality of the operations. Its operations consist of *musharakah*, *mudarabah*, *murabahah* and *qard hasan*. Authorized capital was US$500 million and paid-up capital was $100 million in 1983. Most of the bank's activities consisted of financing short-term projects. However, it had plans to start long-term financing as well. The bank had established thirty-two companies in various development fields. The bank collected and disbursed *zakat* as well.

Faisal Islamic Bank Sudan (FIBS)
Incorporated in August 1977. Has eighteen branches, besides a head office and three subsidiaries for insurance, trade and real estate. Authorized capital, LS100 million. Paid-up capital, LS58.4 million.

al-fakkāk (الفكاك)
Lit: To separate, disjoin and redeem. *Tech*: During fourteenth century Nasrid Spain used in commercial legal transactions to mean redemption of pledges and debts. In Andalus this term was applied to an intermediary who was paid by the relatives of a person in the enemy territory to buy the liberty of the person by paying the required amount to the enemy. Gradually, *al-fakkak* grew in size and functions and started earning commission from

both parties. Other functions performed by him were bargaining of ransoms, trading in silk, lending and dealing in debased currencies, etc. He seems to be the professional money-lender of the then Muslim Spain.

al-falāḥ (الفلاح)

Lit: To thrive, to become happy, to have luck or success. *Tech*: It implies success in the *Akhira* (Hereafter). The *falah* presumes belief in one God, apostlehood of Muhammad, *Akhira* and conformity to the *shariah* in behaviour. The Islamic state has the responsibility of providing for such conditions which may facilitate achievement of the *falah* at individual and collective levels. The spiritual conditions of the *falah* are: humility in prayers, consciousness of God (*taqwa*), remembrance of God, thanksgiving to God, repentance and inner-purification. Economic conditions for the *falah* are: *infaq*, prohibition of *riba*, fulfilment of covenants, avoidance of exploitation, earning livelihood through effort and avoidance of miserliness. Cultural conditions of the *falah* are: system of prayers, pursuit of knowledge, sexual chastity, avoidance of intoxicants and gambling, purification of environments, enjoining of the proper and prohibition of the improper and avoidance of frivolities. Political conditions of the *falah* are: *jihad* and *shura* (consultation). Islamic economics studies the economic conditions of the *falah*. The *falah* is a both-worldly concept. It implies the reconstruction of human character in the light of Islamic values, while providing one a minimum standard of living and clean environments. It also suggests self-respect, self-reliance and a purified soul. Although Islamic economics concentrates on the economic conditions of the *falah*, yet it conceives it as a multi-dimensional concept and remains conscious of its other aspects.

al-fals (pl. fulus) (الفلس)

Designation of the copper coin current in the early centuries of the Islamic era. It was also a small weight equivalent to 0.00082 grams.

al-faqīr **(الفقير)**

Lit: A poor man. *Tech*: Used in the law of *zakat*, for a needy and poor man who has nothing to live on. It includes an unemployed person also. Some jurists think that *al-faqir* is a person who does not have enough to make him liable to pay *zakat*.

al-faqr **(الفقر)**

Lit: Poverty, need, want. *Tech*: A condition of unfulfilled basic needs. It also refers to a condition of lack of contentment, leaving one in a state of greed. But it has a positive connotation as well: indifference towards material endowments despite ability to possess. A natural corollary of *al-faqr* is rough and simple living by one's option (and thus to transfer the surplus to the needy and the poor). In this sense, *al-faqr* is an economic value of Islamic society.

al-faraq **(الفرق)**

A measure equivalent to six *qist* or 3 *sa*. According to most of the jurists it is equal to 6.516 kg. In terms of litres it is 8.244 litres according to most of the jurists but 10.086 according to Hanafites.

farḍ kifāyah **(فرض كفاية)**

Lit: A collective duty upon Muslims, the discharge of which by some of them absolves the rest of its performance, such as *salat al-janazah* or *jihad*. *Tech*: It covers such functions which the community fails to (or cannot) perform and hence are taken over by the Islamic state, such as provision of utilities, building of roads, bridges and canals.

al-farīḍah **(الفريضة)**

Lit: Obligatory. *Tech*: *zakat* obligation on the cattle.

al-farsakh **(الفرسخ)**

Lit: A measure of length, parasang. *Tech*: 1,200 *dhira* equals 3 miles + 720 yards or 5.544 km.

fasād fil'arḍ (فساد فى الأرض)

Lit: Corruption on the earth. It is generally interpreted as highway dacoity, arson, manslaughter, burning of crops and destruction in the society. *Tech*: It also covers such economic behaviour of individuals or policies of the state that cause socio-economic imbalance, poverty, deprivation, retardation in economic growth and unemployment.

al-fāsid (الفاسد)

See *al-batil*.

al-fatah (الفتح)

See *al-ghail*

FIBE

See Faisal Islamic Bank of Egypt.

al-fiqh (الفقة)

Islamic jurisprudence. The science of the *shariah*. It is an important source of Islamic economics.

fi sabil Allah (فى سبيل الله)

Lit: In the name of God. *Tech*: It is one of the eight heads of account on which the *zakat* fund can be expended. It stands for *jihad* in the name of Allah. In a broader sense it includes all those efforts which are carried out to implement Islam, whether it is fighting in the battlefield or by other means.

al-funduq (الفندق)

Lit: A hotel. *Tech*: Specialized large-scale commercial institutions and markets of the mediaeval Islamic period which developed into virtual stock exchanges. They dominated the townscape of great cities in the entire Islamic world.

G

General Agreement for Economic, Technical and Commercial Co-operation among Member States of the Islamic Conference
The agreement was agreed upon by foreign ministers of the member states in 1977. Almost all sates have approved it but not all had ratified it until 1985. The goal is to create a framework for the improved utilization of natural and human resources of the member states. The agreement eases factor movements between member states to promote economic co-operation and development. This is an effort to develop an Islamic common market.

general investment certificates (GIC)
A proposed instrument of *riba*-free banking. The certificate would be offered by commercial banks to savers. Its holder would be entitled to an average rate of profit on all operations of the bank. The GICs would be issued for different maturities ranging between 60 days to 5–10 years. They would also be marketable.

Geniza or Cairo Geniza
Manuscripts mostly in Hebrew characters but in Arabic language originally preserved in a synagogue, partly also in a cemetry of Fustat (old Cairo), the ancient capital of Islamic Egypt. The material originated all over the Mediterranean area and comprises every conceivable type of writing, such as official, business and private correspondence, detailed court records and other judicial documents, contracts, accounts, checks, prescriptions, receipts and inventories, writs of marriage, divorce and manumission, charms, children's exercises and the like. The bulk of the material is of Jewish origin. Manuscripts are preserved in the University Library, Cambridge, the Bodleian Library Oxford, the British Museum, the Jewish Theological Seminary of America New York, the Dropsie College Philadelphia and many other libraries. *Geniza* documents have

thrown new light on the commercial history of Muslims and the Orientalists have used them to draw inferences about Muslim practices.

al-ghabn al-fāḥish (الغبن الفاحش)
Lit: Excessive overcharging or over-pricing. *Tech*: Used for exorbitant or exploitative rate of profit.

al-ghail (الغيل)
Natural water course such as canals, rivulets, streams. Lands irrigated by the water of *al-ghail* are treated as *ushri* lands and pay *ushr* at full rate. *Al-Ghail* are also known as *al-fatah*.

ghair mamlūk (غير مملوك)
Lit: Not owned. See *al-milk al-ammah*.

al-ghallah (الغلة)
Lit: Income, revenue yield, crop. *Tech*: It applies to the yield or rent of land or wages of a labourer or earnings of a servant. It also applies to the coins which are rejected by the treasury but accepted by the merchants in their day-to-day dealings.

al-ghalūl (الغلول)
Lit: Taking a thing and concealing it. *Tech*: Stealing from out of booty before it is distributed by the commander of the army.

al-ghāmir (الغامر)
Lit: Waste, empty (land). *Tech*: Land that is left out of tillage, having formerly been put under the plough. According to some it is the land which is not reached by water so that it has to be irrigated artificially with considerable cost. It may also apply to land, the canal system of which has decayed.

al-ghanā' (al-ghinā') (الغناء)
Lit: Wealth, affluence, sufficiency, adequacy. *Tech*: Relating to the law of *zakat*, a state at which one can dispense with the material help of others. It excludes a person from the category of

beneficiaries of *zakat* and bars him from making any lawful claim to the *zakat* fund. From the traditions of the Prophet, the following stages of *ghana* may be deduced: (a) when a person is in possession of a *nisab* of productive (*nami*) wealth above what one requires to meet, for the whole year, his own needs and of his dependants; (b) when no *zakat* is imposed but, nevertheless, one is not lawfully allowed to accept it—this stage is reached when, in addition to the basic necessities of life, one owns an amount equal to, but not less than 200 *dirhams* of unproductive wealth, such as the possession of clothing, a number of dwelling houses and warehouses, and the possession of abandoned household items and cattle heads, etc.; (c) when it is not desirable for one to stretch forth one's hands in begging but one is lawfully allowed to accept *zakat* if provided. This state is reached when one is in possession of 50 *dirhams* or, one *uqiyah* of silver or is in possession of solvency and livelihood or has sufficient means for the morning and evening meals or when one is physically fit enough to earn one's livelihood.

al-ghanam (الغنم)
Lit: Goats and sheep. *Tech*: It refers to a herd of goats and sheep on which *zakat* is payable.

al-ghānim (الغانم)
Lit: Successful. *Tech*: A soldier of the Muslim army who receives a share from the *ghanimah*.

al-ghanīmah (الغنيمة)
Lit: Whatever is obtained without difficulty. *Tech*: The booty captured in a war with non-Muslims. It includes only moveable property captured from the battle field left behind by the enemy troops. It does not include the land, immoveable property and even moveable property of the enemy not thus captured. Four-fifths of the total *ghanimah* is distributed among those who participated in the war and one-fifth is the share of the *bait al-mal*. See also *khumus*.

al-gharar (الغرر)
Lit: Hazard, chance or risk (*khatar*). *Tech*: Sale of a thing which is not present at hand; or the sale of a thing whose *aqibah* (consequence, outcome) is not known; or a sale involving risk or hazard in which one does not know whether it will come to be or not, such as a fish in the water or a bird in the air.

al-gharb (الغرب)
Lit: A large bucket. *Tech*: A large bucket tied to the camel or bullock working on a well to irrigate land. Half *ushr* is levied on such lands. This bucket is also known as *al-rasha*.

al-ghārim (pl. ghārmīn) (الغارم)
Lit: Debtor. *Tech*: Relating to the law of *zakat*, a debtor who does not own a *nisab* over and above his debt. It is one of the eight heads of account on which *zakat* can be expended. It means that the *zakat* can be expended to pay off the debt of a person, who if he pays off his own debt from his assets, is left with less than the *nisab*. All such persons can claim help from the *zakat*. According to some jurists, it includes not only those who are unable to pay off the debts they incur for their personal purposes, but also includes those who incur debts in the interests of the society, such as in making reconciliation and peace between feuding persons or tribes or in standing security in the lawful interest of another person. According to some it also includes those on whom a calamity has befallen such as destruction of property by fire. In interest-free banking model, it has been suggested by some, that the *zakat* can be utilized to compensate such bad-debt losses to the bank which have been caused by the inability of the debtor to pay back the amount taken.

al-ghaṣb (الغصب)
Lit: To usurp. *Tech*: Forcibly taking possession of the property of someone else. The jurists have dealt with the question of liability of the usurper in detail.

good management fee

Relating to the *musharakah* financing by banks in Pakistan, it is a fee payable to the client where the projected profit percentage of the venture is more than the maximum of the return rate laid down by the State Bank of Pakistan. Where the actual profit is equal to the provisional rate of profit, the bank shall not allow any good management fee to the client.

Gulf Co-operation Council (GCC)

Bahrain, Kuwait, Oman, Qatar, Saudi Arabia and UAE set up the GCC in 1981. In 1983, they abolished custom duties on intra-GCC trade in agricultural and animal products processed from locally obtained materials and on manufactured goods made from imported raw materials if domestic value added constituted at least 40 per cent of the cost of the finished product and the nationals owned 51 per cent of the equity of the firm producing it.

al-ghurm (الغرم)

Lit: Damage, loss. *Tech*: Liability of a debtor for any loss or damage caused by any factor other than a crime or dishonesty on the part of the debtor. It also applies to the payment and performance bond provided by a contractor.

H

al-ḥabbah (الحبة)

Lit: Grain, granule. *Tech*: A weight of six grains of barley is 0.062 grams.

al-ḥabs (pl. aḥbās; also ḥubs, ḥubūs) (الحبس)

Inalienable property, the yield of which is devoted to pious purposes; religious bequest.

al-ḥabīs (pl. ḥubus) (الحبيس)

An alternate term used for al-*waqf*, mostly in North Africa.

al-ḥadīth (pl. ahādīth) (الحديث)
Lit: Speech, conversation. *Tech*: Speech, action, habits and events of the Prophet's life codified by his companions and enlarged and revised by later Muslims. There is a large collection of *ahadith*, the most authentic of which have been recorded in the six books compiled by Bukhari, Muslim, Tirmadhi, Abu Dawud, Ibn Majah and Nisai. These books are known as *sihah sittah*, the 'six correct compilations'. There are other collections also, the compilers of which are not regarded with comparable grace. In the process of collection and compilation of *ahadith*, a detailed art of evaluation of *hadith* developed. Later on all *ahadith* were graded according to the criteria accepted by the majority. *Hadith* is the second source of law in Islam. In Islamic economics as well, the contents of authentic *ahadith* are accepted as a valid source.

al-ḥāfiẓ (الحافظ)
A person employed to keep guard on *zakat* assets. He is included in the category of *amilin* and paid out of *zakat* funds.

al-ḥājjah al-aṣlīyyah (الحاجة الاصلية)
Lit: Basic needs. *Tech*: In relation to the law of *zakat*, the shariah has exempted those assets which are required to fulfill one's basic needs. Also spoken with regard to economic role of the Islamic state. The Islamic state is responsible to provide for the basic needs of all citizens, should some of them fall short of the means.

al-ḥajjājī (الحجاجى)
A grain measure. One *al-hajjaji* equals one *al-qafiz al-hajjaji*, 8 *ratls* or 3.27 kilograms.

al-ḥajr (الحجر)
Lit: To deny access, to stop, to detain. *Tech*: To deny the right to make use of one's own assets, in case one's activities are harmful for the collective good or one is unable to use them properly because of lunacy, minority, indebtedness or slavery. It includes

restrictions on extravagance and squandering of wealth on frivolous objects. This law gives wide powers to the state for intervening into individual freedom. This executive authority, however, remains bound by the superiority of the judiciary, where one can resort to for seeking justice, in case the state has exceeded its limits.

al-ḥalāl (الحلال)

Lit: Permissible. The concept of *al-halal* has spiritual overtones. There are activities, professions, contracts and transactions which have been explicitly prohibited (*al-haram*) by the Quran or the sunnah. Barring them (i.e. al-haram), all other activities, professions, transactions, etc., are *al-halal* (permissible). This is one of the distinctive features of the Islamic economics vis-a-vis Western economics where no such concept exists. In Western economics, all activities are judged on the touchstone of economic utility. In Islamic economics other factors, mostly moral and spiritual are also involved. An activity may be economically sound, but may not be allowed in the Islamic society if it is not permitted by the shariah.

ḥaly al-maḥẓūr (الحلى المحظور)

Lit: Prohibited ornaments. *Tech*: Relating to the law of *zakat*, it refers to gold or silver cast into utensils or decoration pieces.

al-ḥamālah (الحمالة)

A bloodwit or a debt, an obligation or a responsibility that must be paid, discharged or performed, taken upon himself by a person for others.

al-ḥamūlah (الحمولة)

Lit: Transport charges. *Tech*: Transport charges of the tax on agricultural land paid by the tiller in kind. During mediaeval Islam the peasant was supposed to pay the tax in cash or deliver the crop at the place designated by the government, bearing the transport charges himself. The jurists contended that this was an undesirable practice and the peasants should be exempted from it.

al-ḥaqal (الحقل)
See *al-muhaqalah*.

ḥaqq bait al-māl (حق بيت المال)
Lit: What is due to the state treasury. *Tech*: It refers to the taxation system in Ummayyad Iraq in which the tiller held the land under more than one lord, i.e., the local feudal lord and the state. So the term *haqq bait al-mal* was used in distinction with *haqq al-dihqanah*, which meant what was due to the local feudal lord.

ḥaqq al-dihqānah (حق الدهقانة)
See *haqq bait al-mal*.

ḥaqq-al-ʾirtifāq (حق الارتفاق)
Lit: The right of utilization or easement. *Tech*: The right to derive benefits gratis from the immovable property of someone else. This right has been recognized by the shariah in the spirit of generosity which members of a community should display about each other. Following are important classes of this haqq. (a) The right to obtain drinking water for self and animals from the canal privately owned by someone else, known as *haqq al-shurb*. (b) The right to fetch canal water from across the land owned by someone else, known as *haqq al-majra*. (c) The right to drain out waste water over the property of someone else, known as *haqq al-masil*. (d) The right of access to one's own property across the property of someone else, known as *haqq al-murur*. (e) The right of stopping the neighbour from carrying out such modifications in his property that may cause harm to oneself, known as *haqq al-jiwar*.

ḥaqq al-jiwār (حق الجوار)
See *haqq al-irtifaq*.

ḥaqq al-majrā (حق المجرى)
See *haqq al-irtifaq*.

ḥaqq al-marūr (حق المرور)
See *haqq al-irtifaq*.

ḥaqq al-masīl (حق المسيل)
See *haqq al-irtifaq*.

ḥaqq al-shufʿah (حق الشفعة)
Lit: Right of pre-emption. *Tech*: A right to acquire by purchase an immovable property in preference to other persons by reason of such right.

ḥaqq al-shurb (حق الشرب)
See *haqq al-irtifaq*.

al-ḥarām (الحرام)
Lit: Prohibited, unlawful. See *al-halal*.

al-ḥarth (الحرث)
Relating to the law of *zakat*, it refers to agricultural produce in general.

hāshimī (هاشمى)
A measure for grain prevalent in the Abbaside period. One sealed (makhtum) hashimi equals 8 *ratls* or 3.27 kilograms.

al-ḥawālah (الحوالة)
Lit: Bill of exchange, promissory note, cheque, draft. *Tech*: A debtor passes on the responsibility of payment of his debt to a third party who owes the former a debt. Thus the responsibility of payment is ultimately shifted to a third party. *Al-hawalah* is a mechanism which can be usefully employed for settling international accounts by book transfer. This obviates, to a large extent, the necessity of physical transfer of cash. The term was also used, historically, in the public finance during the Abbaside

period to refer to cases where the state treasury could not meet the claims presented to it and it directed its claimants to occupy a certain region for a certain period and procure their claims themselves by taxing the people. This method was also known as *tasabbub*. The taxes collected and transmitted to the central treasury were known as *mahmul* (i.e. carried to the treasury) while those assigned to the claimants or provinces were known as *musabbab*.

al-ḥawālah ʿala al-barīʾ (الحوالة على البرىء)

Endorsement of one's debt to a third party who is not a debtor of the person endorsing the debt. The term has been applied in the model of *riba*-free banking by some. An obvious example is the case where a cheque is written in favour of a third party and drawn upon the bank which does not have a credit balance of the cheque-writer in its books.

al-ḥawālah ʿala al-maqrūḍ (الحوالة على المقروض)

Endorsement of one's debt to a third party who is a debtor of the person endorsing the debt. The term has been used in the model of *riba*-free banking by some. An obvious example is the case where a cheque is written in favour of a third party and drawn upon the bank which has a credit balance of the cheque-writer in the books of the bank.

al-ḥawāmil (الحوامل)

Used in the law of *zakat* for those animals engaged in carriage of goods.

al-ḥawl (الحول)

Period for which *zakat* (*ushr*) becomes due. In case of cash, gold, silver, stock-in-trade and cattle, it is one year and in case of agricultural and mineral produce, it is as and when the produce is available.

ʿal-ḥāzir (الحازر)

An estimator for the green fruits and vegetables employed by the tax departments during the Abbaside period.

al-hibah (الهبة)

Lit: Gift, donation. *Tech*: Transfer of a determinate property (*mal*) without any material consideration. Muslims have been exhorted by the Prophet to donate gifts to others. This is one of the important values of a Muslim society. It is intended to cultivate love and co-operation among citizens rather than rivalry and competition.

hibah bil ʿiwaḍ (هبة بالعوض)

A gift in exchange of gift without the exchange being a condition of the gift. It is a simple gift transaction except that revocation of gift cannot take place.

hibah bi sharṭ al-ʿiwaḍ

A gift on condition of an exchange. For instance, A gives a house to B on condition that B will give to A a garden belonging to B. Such a transaction partakes of the nature both of gift and sale. It is regarded as a gift in its inception, so that it will not be valid with respect to an undivided property (*musha*) and neither party will acquire any right in the thing given to him before delivery of seisin. After delivery of possession by each party the transaction has all the incidents of a sale, so that neither party can revoke his act; the right of pre-emption will attach to the property and either party can return for defect the article which he has received.

al-ḥilm (الحلم)

Lit: Being mild, gentle, clement. Restraining oneself at a time when the spirit is roused to anger. *Tech*: Relating to mutual relations of trade, employment and *qard* (debt), the aggrieved party is required to keep his cool and show *al-hilm* towards others. It is one of the values of Muslim society.

al-ḥimā (الحمى)

Lit: Grazing lands for the cattle. *Tech*: Those pieces of land which are meant for the grazing of state cattle. On these plots individual ownership is not permitted. The Islamic state has an inherent right to declare any remote or commonly used meadow as *al-hima*. But the state cannot appropriate any individual's property for this purpose.

al-ḥimāyah (الحماية)
See *al-taljiah*.

al-ḥiml (الحمل)
Relating to the law of *zakat*, it is a measure of weight equivalent to one *wasq* or 60 *sa*. According to Hanafites it is equal to 192.69 kilograms or 201.72 litres, while the rest of the jurists consider it equal to 130.32 kilograms or 164.88 litres.

al-ḥiqqah (الحقة)
Relating to the *nisab* for *zakat*, a young (grown up) she-camel in her fourth year. Such a she-camel is fit for becoming pregnant and for carrying a load.

al-ḥisbah (الحسبة)
Lit: Reward, calculation. *Tech*: An institution throughout Muslim history to implement what is proper and to prevent what is improper. The main role of the *hisbah* remained the control of markets. The department of *hisbah* used to have a head with technical staff well-versed in various products and processes. The department was often assisted by the police. The *hisbah* staff used to summon recalcitrant debtors to pay their debts, prevent too-heavy charges required by ships and street porters, destroy houses that were near falling off and control weights and measures.

al-hiyal (sing. hila) (الحيل)
Lit: Artifices, strategic, tricks, devices.

al-hubs (pl. ahbas) (الحبس)
An alternate term used for *al-waqf*, mostly in North Africa.

hulwān al-kāhin (حلوان الكاهن)
Lit: Sweets offered to a sorcerer. *Tech*: The earnings of a fortune-teller in whatever form they may be.

I

al-ʿīarah (الإعارة)
Lending some durable article for temporary use.

IBID
See Islamic Bank International of Denmark.

ibn labūn (ابن لبون)
Relating to the *nisab* for *zakat*, a two-year-old he-camel.

ibn makhāḍ (ابن مخاض)
Relating to the *nisab* for *zakat*, one-year-old he-camel.

ibn al-sabil (إبن السبيل)
Lit: Traveller. *Tech*: One of the eight heads of account on which *zakat* may be expended. The *zakat* may be spent to help a traveller if he has fallen short of funds during the journey even though he may be a rich person.

al-ʿibrah (العبرة)
During the Abbaside period, it referred to the average rate of tax for each locality or area. The average was calculated on the basis of the lowest and the highest revenues of the previous few years.

'ibtighā' faḍl Allah (إبتغاء فضل الله)
Quranic term for economic struggle. It implies that struggle to earn livelihood is a part of the overall struggle to achieve *al-falah* in the Hereafter. Whatever one earns is a *nimah* (gift) or *fadl* from Allah and one will have to account for it on the day of judgement.

ICCICE
Islamic Chamber of Commerce, Industry and Commodity Exchange. Established in 1978 at Karachi, as an organ of the OIC, it promotes industrial co-operation by Islamic joint ventures.

ICDT
Islamic Centre for Development of Trade. Established in 1981 at Casablanca as an organ of the OIC it aims at regular commercial contacts and promotes harmonization of commercial and investment policies of Islamic countries.

ICECSA
The Islamic Commission for Economic, Cultural and Social Affairs. Formed in 1976, it is an organ of the OIC which reports to the Conference of Foreign Ministers. It superseded the Permanent Commission of Economic Experts and the Commission of Economic Experts and Representatives.

ICVTTR
Islamic Centre for Vocational and Technical Training and Research. It was established at Dhaka in 1978 as an organ of the OIC. It helps to meet the demand for technically qualified manpower in the Islamic countries.

'iḍā'at al-māl (اضاعة المال)
Lit: Wasting of wealth, squandering. *Tech*: Dissipation of wealth in any manner not allowed by the shariah including dumping of goods in the sea to keep scarcity in the market. Other examples are setting on fire or destroying goods or assets in a selfish manner.

IDB
See Islamic Development Bank Jeddah.

IFH
See Islamic Finance House.

IFHUH
Islamic Finance House Universal Holding (formerly Islamic Banking System), Luxembourg.

IFSTAD
Islamic Foundation for Science, Technology and Development. Established in 1978 at Jeddah, as an organ of the OIC, it collects and disseminates information on research facilities of the Muslim world and co-ordinates activities in the field of science and technology.

al-iḥrāz (الإحراز)
Relating to the law of ownership, it refers to securing or taking possession of things not already owned by another.

al-ihsān (الإحسان)
Lit: Beneficence. *Tech*: *al-Ihsan* is to accept readily and ungrudgingly while receiving, a smaller share than what is due and to give, while paying back, a larger share than what is due. *Al-Ihsan* is an important value of Muslim society. It is over and above the legal equitability of the *al-adl* and is practised voluntarily.

al-'iḥtikār (الإحتكار)
The hoarding and corner-marketing of commodities of any kind, particularly foodstuffs, with a view to creating an artificial scarcity and rise in price.

'iḥyā' al-mawāt (إحياء الموات)
Lit: Revival of dead lands. *Tech*: Development of ownerless lands (*al-mawat*) to make them productive. Also see *al-ard al-mawat*.

'iḥyā' al-tamlīk (إحياء التمليك)
The process of development of a dead land which entitles a person to claim ownership of the land. It includes cultivation, plantation and irrigation, etc., on this land.

IIIBE
See International Institute of Islamic Banking and Economics.

al-ījār (الإيجار)
A class of privileged landlords who were not subjected to arbitrary taxation. Their taxes were fixed once for all. They were not increased on any pretext nor was a concession given to them if the land became waste or the crop was destroyed. The privilege was enjoyed by the landlord and his posterity.

al-ʾijārah (الإجاره)
Lit: Letting on lease. *Tech*: Sale of a definite usufruct in exchange for definite reward. But it is commonly used for wages. Also it refers to a contract of land lease at a fixed rent payable in cash. It is contrary to *muzarah* when rent is fixed as a certain percentage of the produce of land. It also refers to a mode of financing adopted by Islamic banks. It is an arrangement under which the Islamic bank leases equipment, a building or other facility to a client against an agreed rental. The rent is so fixed that the bank gets back its original investment plus a profit on it.

al-ijārah wal-ʾiqtinā (الإجاره والاقتناء)
A mode of financing adopted by Islamic banks. It is a contract under which the Islamic bank finances equipment, building or other facility for the client against an agreed rental together with an undertaking from the client to make additional payments in an account which will eventually permit the client to purchase the equipment or the facility. The rental as well as the purchase price is fixed in such a manner that the bank gets back its principal sum along with some profit which is usually determined in advance.

al-ʾijārah bi sharṭ al-tamlīk (الإجاره بشرط التمليك)
It is leasing of property to a party on the condition that it shall be sold to him after an agreed period on terms and conditions mentioned in the agreement of lease.

al-'ijmā' (الإجماع)
Lit: Consensus. *Tech*: Consensus of the jurists (*mujtahidin*) on a certain question in a certain age. It is of two broad types: (a) *ijma qauli*, in which all the jurists give their opinion explicitly; (b) *ijma sukuti*, in which some express their opinion but others do not oppose it.

al-'ijtihād (الاجتهاد)
Lit: Effort, exertion, industry, diligence. *Tech*: Endeavour of a jurist to derive or formulate a rule of law on the basis of evidence found in the sources.

al-'ikhtilāṭ (الاختلاط)
Relating to the law of partnership, it refers to the intermingling of two investments so that they cannot be distinguished any more.

al-'iktināz (الاكتناز)
Lit: To accumulate, to amass, to hide wealth. *Tech*:. Accumulation of wealth without paying *zakat* due on it. It also refers to unproductive accumulation of wealth.

'iktisāb al-ḥalāl (اكتساب الحلال)
Struggle for earning livelihood through lawful means. It is an important value of Muslim society.

'ilja' lands
See *al-taljiah*.

'ilm 'al-iqtiṣād al-'islāmī (علم الإقتصاد الإسلامى)
Lit: Islamic Economics. *Tech*: It has been differently defined by different scholars. Some of the definitions are (a) Islamic economics is the knowledge and application of injunctions and rules of.the shariah that prevent injustice in the acquisition and disposal of material resources in order to provide satisfaction to human beings and enable them to perform their obligations to Allah and the society. (b) Islamic economics aims at the study of

human *falah* achieved by organizing the resources of earth on the basis of co-operation and participation. (c) Islamic economics is the study of the behaviour of Muslims who organize the resources, which are a trust, to achieve *falah*.

ʿilm tadbir al-manzil (علم تدبير المنزل)

The science of economics, referred to in mediaeval Muslim sources. The goal of this knowledge was management of the household. The economy of the home included the totality of all its human relationships. Home economy was not formed by the market but concentrated on home and farm. It united ethics, economics and politics. Despite an urge for gain, the motives for enterprise were different from the factory production of modern capitalism. The *ilm tadbir al-manzil* studied the concept of the 'whole house' as distinct from modern economics which emerges from a market economy and concentrates on material aspects of life.

al-ʾiltizām (إلتزام)

See *al-muqataa*.

al-īmān (الإيمان)

Lit: Faith. *Tech*: Faith in the oneness of God, in Muhammad's apostlehood and his finality, in the day of the Judgement, in the unseen matters like angels, revelation, paradise, hell, etc.

ʾimān bil ghaib (إيمان بالغيب)

Lit: Faith in the Unseen. *Tech*: A Muslim's faith in God, prophets, revelation, paradise, hell, angels, etc. *Iman bil ghaib* is a cornerstone of the value system which governs Muslim society. It induces a behaviour which is richly imbued in the obedience of God and the Prophet, and a high sense of accountability on the day of Judgement.

al-ʿinān al-ʿāmmah (العنان العامه)

Relating to the law of partnership, a type of *shirkah al-inan*, comprehending a variety of business operations as against *al-inan al-khassah* which is limited to a single purchase and resale.

al-ʿinan al-khāṣṣah **(العنان الخاصه)**
See *al-inan al-ammah*

al-ʾinfāq **(الإنفاق)**
Lit: Spending, expenditure. *Tech*: Spending to seek Allah's pleasure, whether to discharge a liability or voluntarily, on the poor, needy or to meet social needs. *Al-infaq* also covers one's expenditure on one's self, family and relations.

International Institute of Islamic Banking and Economics (IIIBE)
The IIIBE was established on 25 March 1981 by the DMI in Cyprus. Its objectives were to train people for the growing network of Islamic banks and to undertake research in Islamic economics. The Institute was closed in 1984.

al-ʾiqālah **(الإقالة)**
Lit: Cancellation, revocation. *Tech*: Cancellation or revocation of a contract of sale. There is a detailed code on *al-iqalah* in the texts of jurisprudence.

al-ʾiqtāʿ **(الإقطاع)**
Lit: The act of bestowing a *qatiah* (a cut-off piece). *Tech*: A piece of land donated by the state in the public interest subject to state taxes to a person for self-cultivation. Sometimes the ownership is passed on to the donee but at other times only the right to derive benefit is granted and the ownership remains with the state.

ʾiqṭāʿ al-ʾijārah **(إقطاع الإجارة)**
A piece of land donated to someone by the state on the basis of rent. The ownership rights remain with the state which can always dispose of it in any other manner. See *iqta al-tamlik*.

ʾiqṭāʿ al-ʾirfāq **(إقطاع الإرفاق)**
See *al-irfaq*.

'iqṭā' al-'istighlāl (إقطاع الإستغلال)

Assigning of tax-revenue to a person by the state relating to a particular land or area. The donee is authorized to collect *kharaj* from the people and to keep it with himself. He is not required to deposit it with the public treasury. In this case, the land itself is not subject of donation. This type of donation was prevalent during mediaeval Islam.

'iqṭā' al-ma'din (إقطاع المعدن)

Those pieces of land donated to someone by the state which contain mineral deposits.

'iqṭā' al-tamlīk (إقطاع التمليك)

A piece of land donated to someone by the state on a permanent basis without any liability for tax. Such an *iqta* is treated as private property of the person to whom donated. The granted land could be dead land (*mawat*), arable land (*amir*) or land containing minerals (*maadin*).

al-'iqtiṣād (الإقتصاد)

Lit: To adopt a middle course. *Tech*: To be moderate between *israf* and *bukhl*. *Iqtisad* is one of the important values of Muslim society.

al-'iqtiyāt (الإقتيات)

Lit: Food-stuff. *Tech*: Relating to the law of *riba al-fadl*. According to some jurists, one of the causes for the prohibition of *riba al-fadl* lies in the articles of exchange being food-stuff (*al-iqtiyat*).

al-'irfāq (الإرفاق)

Concessions in public property such as market places or inaccessible mines given to individuals on payment of certain duties or taxes. They are also known as *iqta al-irfaq*.

'irq al-ẓālim (عرق الظالم)

Unlawful cultivation of a land owned by another person.

al-'irṣādāt (الإِرصادات)

Trusts formed out of state lands for the benefit of those who are entitled to such benefits from the *bait al-mal*. They are governed by the law of *waqf*.

IRTI

Islamic Research and Training Institute. Established by the Islamic Development Bank, Jeddah, in 1981, it conducts theoretical and conceptional research in the field of Islamic economics and law as well as policy-oriented research regarding Islamic banking, development finance and economic co-operation among Islamic countries.

'irtifāq (إرتفاق)

Lit: Public utility. See *haqq al-irtifaq*.

Islamic Bank Bangladesh Limited (IBBL)

Incorporated on 13 March 1983. Besides a head office, it has sixteen branches in Bangladesh. Authorized capital, Taka500 million. Paid-up capital, Taka79.5 million.

Islamic Bank for Western Sudan (IBWS)

Incorporated in 1981. Has a branch at Nyala. Paid-up capital, LS25 million.

Islamic Bank International of Denmark (IBID)

Islamic Bank International of Denmark is the first fully fledged Islamic bank in Europe. The capital is 30 million Danish kroner. Its main aim is to promote the business of Scandinavian companies connected with the Islamic world, to serve other Islamic banks and to provide normal banking activities. IBID claims to operate on a non-interest basis. The parent company, Islamic Banking System (IBS), has among its shareholders the Kuwait Finance House, Abu Dhabi's Ministry of *Awqaf* and prominent Muslim individuals.

Islamic Banking System (IBS)

See Islamic Bank International of Denmark.

Islamic Centre for Development of Trade
See ICDT.

Islamic Centre for Vocational And Technical Training
See ICVTT.

Islamic Chamber of Commerce, Industry and Commodity Exchange
See ICCICE.

Islamic Commission for Economic, Cultural and Social Affairs
See ICECSA.

Islamic Development Bank Jeddah
Established as a result of a decision by the Organization of the Islamic Conference in 1975, the IDB is owned by forty-one member countries of the OIC. The authorized capital is 2 billion Islamic dinars (equivalent to 2 billion SDRs). The subscribed capital of the Bank at the end of 1401H was 1822.67 million Islamic dinars. All member countries have subscribed to the capital but the major contributors are Saudi Arabia, Libya, Kuwait and the UAE. The bank provides development finance to the Muslim countries on the basis of *musharakah*, *mudarabah* and *qard hasan*. The bank claims to follow the principles of the shariah in all its business. The bank also promotes the establishment of Islamic banks and has arrangements for in-house research on Islamic banking and economics. See Islamic Research and Training Institute or IRTI.

Islamic dinar (ID)
Currency used to denominate share capital of Islamic Development Bank, Jeddah. Officially one ID equals one SDR of IMF.

Islamic Foundation for Science and Technology
See IFSTAD.

Islamic Takafol Company, Luxembourg
Incorporated on 28 December 1982. A subsidiary of DMI, carries out Islamic insurance business. Paid-up capital, US$3 million.

al-'isrāf (الإسراف)
Lit: Intemperance, immoderateness, exaggeration, waste. *Tech*: Covers (a) spending on lawful objects but exceeding moderation in quantity or quality; (b) spending on superfluous objects while necessities are unfulfilled; (c) spending on objects which are incompatible with the economic standard of the majority of the population.

al-'istān (الإستان)
Tech: Taxation incumbent on the rural population of fiefs and state domains. It was usually a certain proportion (*muqasamah*) of the produce of land (sometimes to the extent of 50 per cent of the produce). This was a distortion of the taxation system of the shariah which prescribed *ushr* or *kharaj*.

al-'istar (الإستار)
A measure equal to 6.5 dirhams or 19.5 grams.

al-'istidānah (الإستدانة)
Lit: To borrow. *Tech*: Commercial commitment of the *mudarabah* agreement by the agent in excess of the capital invested.

al-'istīfā' (الإستيفاء)
See *diwan al-mal*.

'istīfā al-qard (إستيفاء القرض)
Lit: To receive back the amount of loan in full by the creditor. *Tech*: Used in *riba*-free banking for the operation of a current bank account by cheque.

al-'istīfāf (الإستعفاف)
Tech: To abstain from begging. Begging has been prohibited in the shariah, except (a) when a person is under debt and is not finding

any means to pay it off; (b) when a natural calamity befalls and destroys one's belonging; (c) when one is poverty-stricken and three persons of his community testify to it. In all these cases one may beg only to the extent of meeting the above needs. In no case is this to be a regular source of income.

al-ʾistighnāʾ (الإستغناء)

Lit: Being rich. *Tech*: Feeling rich and independent and thinking oneself capable of getting along without God and His commandment. This is an improper attitude and has been condemned in the Quran.

al-ʾistiḥsān (الإستحسان)

Relating to the sources of Islamic law, it is a deviation, on a certain issue, from the rule of a precedent to another rule for a more relevant legal reason that requires such deviation.

al-ʾistiqrād (الإستقراض)

Lit: To raise a loan. *Tech*: In a contract of *mudarabah* or *shirkah*, the *rabb al-mal* or other partners may authorize the *mudarib* or working partners to raise loan in cash for business over and above the business capital.

al-istiṣlāh (الإستصلاح)

Relating to the sources of Islamic law, it is the unprecedented judgement motivated by public interest to which neither the Quran nor the sunnah explicitly refer.

al-ʾitāwah (الإتاوه)

Originally a due imposed on foreign traders in return for protection or a tax paid by strangers and all such Arabs whom no alliance had attached to the Qurashite clans. It was paid in money and did not take into account the value of the land. In the later usage it became a gross amount that was paid according to an agreement.

J

al-jadhʿa (الجذع)

Lit: Young man. *Tech*: Relating to the law of *zakat*, it refers to a she-camel in the fifth year. It is also spoken for a lamb of six months or more.

jāgīr (Urdu)

A piece of land donated to a person by the state. The owner enjoys absolute rights on the land on the pattern of feudal lords. The *jagir* is generally perceived as an institution of exploitation. The Islamic concept is, however, different. The Arabic equivalent is *al-iqta*. The donation, in the Islamic state, must be in consideration for significant national service by the donee and the donation must be subject to the laws of the state. By injunctions on other aspects of land tenancy system, possibilities of exploitation have also been minimized. See also *al-iqta*.

al-jahbadh (الجهبذ)

Financial administrator in the Abbaside period responsible for maintaining prescribed standards of fineness and quality of gold content and equivalence of various currencies. He used to be the head of a department called *diwan al-jahbadhah*. He acted like an authorized banker to collect state revenues. He used to prepare and submit periodical statements to the government. Usually the *jahbadh* was a commercial magnate (*tajir*) who owned capital of his own and was able to advance money to the government when the treasury was empty. In some cases the *sahib bait al-mal* and *jahbadh* might be one and the same person. In the same way as there might be a *sahib* for both the *bait al-mal al-ammah* and *bait al-mal al-khassah*, there might be a *jahbadh* for both of them. However, the receipts in kind were kept by the *khazin*.

jalab (جلب)

Lit: Imports. *Tech*: Relating to the law of *zakat*, it refers to the tax-collector's encampment at a particular place and his orders to the assessees to bring their cattle and agricultural produce to his place.

janab (جنب)

Lit: Avoid. *Tech*: Relating to the law of *zakat*, it refers to the avoidance of the tax-payer from the tax-collector by taking away the cattle from their usual location so that the tax collector has to follow them.

al-jarīb (الجريب)

Lit: A patch of arable land. *Tech*: A measure of length and weight. One *jarib* is equal to 1366.0416 sq. meters. As a measure of weight, it is equal to 48 *sa*. According to Hanafi jurists it is equal to 156.552 kilograms or 161.376 litres. But according to other jurists it is equal to 104.256 kilograms or 131.904 litres.

al-jawālī (الجوالى)

Poll-tax imposed upon groups of people who had emigrated from their lands and have taken abode in the towns, and other unsettled people.

al-ji'ālah (الجعالة)

Lit: Stipulated price for performing any service. *Tech*: Applied in the model of *riba*-free banking by some. Bank charges and bank commission has been interpreted to be *al-jialah* of the jurists and thus considered lawful.

al-jibāyah (الجباية)

A comprehensive term expressing all taxes.

al-jizyah (الجزية)

Al-jizyah is mentioned in the Quran (9:29). The word comes from *jaza*, to compensate. In this case it is a compensation for the security and protection the non-Muslims have, without going to war. Historically, the non-Muslims had to pay the *jizyah* on two grounds: for their exemption from the obligation to fight Muslim wars and for exemption from *zakat*. Conversion of a person to Islam freed him from obligation to pay the *jizyah* but subjected him to *jihad* and *zakat*. There were different practices and rates in relation to the *jizyah* determined in the light of the treaty with non-Muslims or the way they became Muslim subjects. It is evident from *ahadith* that *jizyah* was considerably lower than *zakat* on Muslims. Women, children, old people, the poor, disabled and religious leaders were exempted. Similarly, those non-Muslims who opted to serve in the Muslim army were also exempt. Where the *jizyah* was levied in the form of a fixed amount, the terms *kharaj* and *jizyah* were undifferentiated. But as soon as *kharaj* came to mean a land tax and stood in place of *ushr*, *jizyah* was levied in addition and this represented a tax in lieu of *jihad*. In the former case, the *kharaj* means *jizyah* in general, but in the latter case, the *kharaj* simply means land tax; that is to say, that portion of the *jizyah* which is called *kharaj* or the assessment on the produce of the land. *Kharaj* was levied according to the type of land. For example, in Sawad there were three categories of land-tax or *kharaj*: (a) land-tax based on the measured acreage (*al-kharaj ala masahatil ard*); (b) the land tax based on a percentage of the yearly harvest (*al-kharaj ala al-muqasamah*); (c) the fixed amount of money (*al-kharaj ala muqatah*).

Jordan Islamic Bank for Finance and Investment (JIBFI)
Incorporated on 28 November 1978. Paid-up capital, JD6 million.

al-juʿālah **(الجعالة)**
An alternate term for *al-jialah*.

al-juʿl **(الجعل)**
Lit: Pay, wages. *Tech*: Financial levy on Muslims who stay away from war to equip those on military service. In the days of Umar I, married people were taxed to equip the bachelors for war.

al-juzāf **(الجزاف)**
Lit: Purchase of a certain amount of things. *Tech*: Sale transaction of an article without weight, measure or count.

K

al-kafāf **(الكفاف)**
Lit: Sufficiency. *Tech*: That standard of living which provides subsistence and honour in a Muslim society.

al-kafālah **(الكفالة)**
Lit: Suretyship, bail, guarantee. *Tech*: A contract of suretyship in which a person adds to his responsibility or liability on behalf of another person in respect of a demand for something.

al-kafālah bil darak **(الكفالة بالدرك)**
Providing a surety to the buyer for the delivery of a commodity according to specifications. It also refers to the performance bond in a contract.

kafālah bil māl **(الكفالة بالمال)**
Surety for the payment of the price of a commodity bought on credit by another person.

al-kafālah bil taslīm **(الكَفالة بالتسليم)**
Providing a surety for returning a rented asset in proper condition on the termination of the contract of hire.

kafālatul 'awām **(كفالة العوام)**
Lit: Security of people, sponsorship for people. *Tech*: Relating to functions of an Islamic state, it is an important responsibility of the state to ensure for everybody at least those necessities which are essential for the survival and maintenance of human life. It includes food, shelter, dress, and medical aid. But the list will vary according to the socio-economic conditions of the state. The responsibility of the state does not, however, mean provision of these necessities to all citizens except that the state will assist only those who are in need of help due to some physical, social or economic disability.

al-kailjah (الكيلجة)

A measure of weight equivalent to ½ *sa*. According to Hanafites it is equal to 1.680 litres or 1.631 kilograms, whereas according to others it is 1.374 litres and 1.086 kilograms.

al-kalā' (الكلاء)

Lit: Grass, herbage, pasture. *Tech*: Grass grown up naturally. It is one of the three things, along with water and fire, which the Prophet explicitly made a public property and prohibited its monopoly in any form.

al-kalālah (الكلالة)

Relating to the law of inheritance, *al-kalalah* is a person who has neither parents nor children. His wealth is inherited by brothers and sisters in given ratios (Quran 4:176) in the absence of whom it is credited to the *bait al-mal*.

al-kālī' (الكالىء)

Debt whose repayment is postponed.

al-kanz (الكنز)

Lit: A treasure trove. *Tech*: Wealth on which *zakat* has not been paid. It also refers to the unproductive or idle wealth even though *zakat* has been paid on it.

karā' im al-'amwāl (كرائم الأموال)

Relating to the law of *zakat*, it refers to the best of the animals in a flock.

al-kāsib (الكاسب)

Lit: Winner, earner, provider. *Tech*: One who earns by physical or mental labour. Mostly used for the self-employed and business people. It is distinct from *al-ajir* who 'sells' his labour to someone else.

al-kātib (الكاتب)

Lit: Relating to the law of *zakat*, one who acts as scribe or clerk to the *zakat*-collector. He is included in the category of *al-amilīn* and is paid out of *zakat* funds.

al-kayyāl (الكيال)
Tech: Relating to the law of *zakat*, the person who measures off *zakat* dues. He is included in the category of *al-amilin* and is paid out of *zakat* funds.

al-kaẓā'im (الكظائم)
Relating to the law of *ushr*, it refers to such natural watercourses as rivulets, canals and streams.

KFH
See Kuwait Finance House.

al-khafārah (الخفارة)
See *al-taljiah*.

khalaf (خلف)
Lit: Substitute, succession. *Tech*: Relating to the law of ownership, it refers to securing or taking possession of things through succession under the law of inheritance.

al-khalīṭ (الخليط)
Lit: Mixed, blended. *Tech*: A partner (of a business) whose assets cannot be distinctly identified from those of other partners. It contrasts with the *sharik*, whose assets can be identified distinctly. Also, relating to the law of *zakat*, it refers to livestock (*al-mashiyah*) owned by two or more partners where it is not specified which animal belongs to whom.

al-kharāj (الخراج)
Land tax which is levied by the state on the state-owned lands whether the cultivator is a lease-holder or a permanent tenant. The rates can be different in different times. *Al-kharaj* is payable only once in a year, irrespective of the number of crops, except

in the case of *kharaj al-muqasamah* where it is assessed on each crop. See *al-jizyah* also.

al-kharāj bil ḍamān (الخراج بالضمان)

The right to own the yield of a property for which one is responsible in case that property is destroyed. For example, if a person buys a house and then rents it out, but subsequently notices a defect in the house and returns the house to the seller, the seller has no claim on the rent during the period the house remained with the buyer. It states the principle of Islamic jurisprudence that the yield from an asset is for the one who is liable for that asset and one who does not bear the liability has no claim to the yield.

kharāj al-jizyah (خراج الجزية)

See *al-jizyah*.

kharāj al-muqāsamah (خراج المقاسمة)

Land revenue fixed as a percentage of the actual produce of the land as contrary to *al-kharaj al-muwazzafah*, which is fixed in terms of cash.

kharāj al-muqaṭi'ah (خراج المقاطعة)

The amount of *kharaj* fixed as a lump sum to be paid by the vanquished enemy as a result of an agreement. This is in contrast to *al-kharāj al-muqāsamah* and *al-kharāj al-muwazzafah*, which are related to the land and its produce.

kharāj al-muwazzafah (خراج الموظفه)

Land revenue fixed by the state in terms of cash as contrary to *al-kharāj al-muqāsamah* (share-cropping), which depends on the actual produce of the land.

kharāj al-waẓīfah (خراح الوظيفة)

A fixed amount (dirhams or dinars) that is assessed upon the land as tax. Also known as *al-kharaj al-muwazzafah*.

kharāj al-zar' (خراج الذرع)
Rent of land, especially from fiefs (*iqta*) donated to someone.

al-khāriṣ (الخارص)
Relating to the administration of *ushr*; the government official deputed to assess the yield of fruit-trees and crops for levying *ushr*.

al-kharṣ (الخرص)
Assessment of a crop still in growth. Also applied to a sale transaction when the commodity sold is not weighed, measured or counted.

al-khāṣṣah lands
Lands extensively meant for the Prophet in a special way, which are of three types: *Fadak* and the land of *Banu Nadir* and all the goods therein which 'God had returned' to him without war. Second, *safiy* or *safiya* which the Prophet had selected from the booty before it was divided among Muslims. Third, one fifth of the *khumus* of the booty, i.e., 1/25th of the booty.

al-khaṭṭ (الخط)
Lit: Bond or bill of exchange. *Tech*: The term was in vogue during the Muslim period. It was an important banking instrument.

khaṭṭ-al-ṣaraf (خط الصرف)
A credit instrument of mediaeval Spain comparable to cheques of the modern day banks.

al-khāzin (الخازن)
See *bait al-mal*.

al-khibr (الخبر)
See *al-mukhabarah*.

al-khiyānah (الخيانة)
Lit: Faithlessness, breach of faith, deception. *Tech*: It is an important characteristic of the hypocrites and the Muslims are to be

distinguished from non-Muslims by their complete abstinence from *khiyanah*. It is opposite of *amanah* (honest dealing). In economics *khiyanah* refers to all sorts of cheating whether at micro or at macro level.

al-khiyār (الخيار)

Lit: Option *Tech*: A term used to express an option within a certain period after the conclusion of a bargain during which either of the parties may cancel it. Its main types are: *khiyar al-shart*, optional condition, where one of the parties stipulates for a period of three days or less; *khiyar al-aib*, option from defect, the option of dissolving the contract on discovery of defect; *khiyar al-ru yah*, option of inspection, option of rejecting the thing purchased after sight; *khiyar al-tayin*, option of determination, where a person having purchased two or three things of the same kind, stipulates a period to make his selection; *khiyar al-majlis*, the condition of withdrawing from the contract as long as the meetings of the parties continue; *khiyar al-naqd*, where the seller has the option to cancel the contract if the buyer does not pay in cash up to a certain agreed date; *khiyar al-ghubn*, the option of the buyer to cancel the contract if the seller has sold it at a price higher than what evaluators evaluate, *khiyar kashf al-hal*, the buyer's option to cancel the contract on knowing the specifications of the product where a product is sold without specifications; *khiyar al-qabul*, the option to accept or reject a proposal, in a contract of sale, before the proposal is accepted, the option is surrendered by giving acceptance to the proposal; *khiyar al-taghrir*, option to rescind the contract if the seller perpetrates a fraud causing loss to the buyer.

khiyār al-ʿaib (خيار العيب)

See *al-khiyar*.

khiyār al-ghubn (خيار الغبن)

See *al-khiyar*.

khiyār kashf al-ḥāl (خيار كشف الحال)

See *al-khiyar*.

khiyār al-majlis (خيار المجلس)
See *al-khiyar*.

khiyār al-naqd (خيار النقد)
See *al-khiyar*.

khiyār al-qabūl (خيار القبول)
See *al-khiyar*.

khiyār al-ru'yah (خيار الرؤية)
See *al-khiyar*.

khiyār al-sharṭ (خيار الشرط)
See *al-khiyar*.

khiyār al-taghrir (خيار التغرير)
See *al-khiyar*.

khiyār al-ta'yīn (خيار التعيين)
See *al-khiyar*.

khizānah al-māl (خزانة المال)
An alternate term for *bait al-mal*, mostly applied in Muslim Spain.

al-khumus (al-khums) (الخمس)
Lit: one-fifth. *Tech*: It has come to be known as the one-fifth share of the state from the booty. In the early days of Islam, it used to be one of the major sources of public revenue.

khumus al-khumus (خمس الخمس)
One-fifth of the *khumus* or 1/25th of the entire booty. The Prophet divided the *khumus* into five shares: Allah and His Prophet, relatives of the Prophet, orphans, *masakin* and travellers.

kirā' al-arḍ (كراء الارض)

Lit: Rent of land. *Tech*: Rent of public lands received in the *bait al-mal*. It is an important source of revenue in an Islamic economy with agricultural bias.

al-kis al-wahid (الكيس الواحد)

Lit: Single purse. *Tech*: Relating to partnership business, most probably the usage owes its origin to the single purse of money which the partners used to operate.

al-kurr (الكر)

A measure for wheat employed in Iraq (tenth and eleventh centuries A.D.) equivalent to 720 *sa* or 12 *wasqs*. According to Hanafites, it is equivalent to 2348.28 kilograms or 2420.64 litres, while according to other jurists it is equivalent to 1563.84 kilograms or 1978.56 litres.

al-kurra al-mu'addal (الكر المعدل)

Most commonly used measure of wheat in Iraq (tenth and eleventh centuries A.D.), equivalent to 7200 *ratls*.

al-kurr al-qanqal (الكر القنقل)

A wheat measure employed in Iraq (tenth and eleventh centuries A.D.) equivalent to 3000 *ratls*.

Kuwait Finance House

It was established by the government of Kuwait on 23 March 1977. It started its operations on 31 August 1978 with 49 per cent shares held by the government and 51 per cent by private individuals. KFH is engaged in banking, insurance, real estate, share dealings and general trade on profit and loss sharing basis. The KFH also undertakes social operations, such as distribution of *zakat*, building of schools, mosques and clinics. It also provides *qard hasan*.

L

LC
See *leasing certificates*

LDT
Licensed Deposit Taker. In Britain the law does not allow Islamic banking. However, the Bank of England has allowed certain institutions to accept deposits only. These institutions intend to operate on the principles of the shariah.

leasing certificates (LC)
A proposed instrument of *riba*-free banking. The certificate would be offered by commercial banks to savers for investing their funds in lease operations.

lending ratio
The ratio of funds set aside for interest-free loans with total demand deposit in an Islamic bank.

al-luqaṭah
Lit: Article or a thing found. *Tech*: Property which a person finds lying upon the ground and takes away for the purpose of preserving it in the manner of a trust.

M

mā' al-bahr (ماء البحر)
Water of the ocean to which every person has an equal right.

al-mā' al-'idd (الماء العد)
Lit: Water which gushes forth by itself. *Tech*: Relating to the law of *iqta*, a place which contains a source of water gushing forth naturally and being accessible to common people. It cannot be donated as *iqta* to anyone. The Prophet withdrew salt layers of Maarib after granting them as *iqta* on this plea.

mā' al-kharaj (ماء الخراج)
Water of canals dug by non-Muslims but now within the Muslim territory. Lands irrigated by this water are subject to *kharaj*.

mā' al-nahr (ماء النهر)
The water of large rivers from which every person has an equal right to drink and also conditional right to irrigate his lands.

mā' al-shurb (ماء الشرب)
The water used for irrigating land. A person is entitled to dig a canal from the river to irrigate his lands, provided it is not detrimental to the interests of others. In case of dispute, there are explicit instructions for courts to adjudicate.

mā' al-ʿushr (ماء العشر)
The water of wells, springs, streams, rivers and rainfall. Lands irrigated by water of such natural sources are subject to *ushr*.

al-madhrūʿāt (المذروعات)
Things which are estimated by linear measurement, such as a yard of cloth.

al-mā'dhūn (المأذون)
The slave whose owner has granted him permission to engage in trade.

al-madī (المدى)
Lit: A dry measure. *Tech*: One *madi* is equal to 22.5 *sa*. According to Hanafites, one *madi* is equal to 73.384 kilograms or 75.645 litres, while other jurists consider it equal to 48.870 kilograms or 61.83 litres.

al-maʿdin al-baṭin (المعدن الباطن)
The mineral deposits which are hidden in the earth and their excavation requires much labour such as gold, silver, oil, gas, etc.

al-maʿdin al-ẓahir (المعدن الظاهر)
The mineral deposits, such as salt, graphite, etc., which are on the surface of the earth and do not involve much labour in excavation.

maghribī dīnār (مغربى دينار)
Dinars minted by the Fatimides in Egypt and in Syria.

al-maḥmūl (المحمول)
Lit: Something carried. *Tech*: In the Abbaside period, taxes collected from the provinces and carried to the central treasury as against *musabbab*; taxes assigned to the provinces or to certain claimants against central treasury.

al-maḥrūm (المحروم)
Lit: deprived, bereaved. *Tech*: A poor man who has been deprived of means of sustenance and requires help for personal maintenance. The Quran speaks of the share of the *mahrum* in the wealth of the rich.

al-maisir (الميسر)
Lit: An ancient Arabian game of chance played with arrows without heads and feathering, for stakes of slaughtered and quartered camels. *Tech*: It came to be identified for all types of gambling.

majālis al-ʾaṣl (مجالس الأصل)
See *diwan* and *diwan al-kharaj*.

majālis al-ḥawādith (مجالس الحوادث)
See *diwan al-nafaqat*.

majālis al-ḥisab (مجالس الحساب)
See *diwan al-kharaj*.

majālis al-ʾinzāl (مجالس الإنزال)
See *diwan al-nafaqat*.

majālis al-jārī (مجالس الجارى)
See *diwan al-nafaqat*.

majālis al-jaysh (مجالس الجيش)
See *diwan al-kharaj*.

majālis al-sudān (مجالس السودان)
See *diwan al-kharaj*.

majālis al-tafṣīl (مجالس التفصيل)
See *diwan al-kharaj*.

al-makhzan (المخزن)
Public treasury in fourteenth century Muslim Spain.

al-makīlāt (المكيلات)
Things which were ordinarily sold by measurement of capacity, such as wheat and barley. See also *al-mauzunat*.

al-maks (المكس)
Tax, more particularly excise or sales tax. See also *sahib al-maks*.

al-makkūk (المكوك)
A measure equivalent to 1.5 *sa*. According to Hanafites, it is equivalent to 4.892 kilograms or 5.043 litres, while other jurists consider it equivalent to 3.258 kilograms or 4.122 litres.

al-māl (pl. al-amwal) (المال)
Lit: Wealth. *Tech*: Something which can be hoarded or secured for use at the time of need. There are three attributes of *al-mal*: that it must have some value, that it must be a thing the benefit of which is permitted under the Islamic law and that it must be possessed. It is of two kinds in respect of form: *al-mal al-batin* (hidden) and *al-mal al-zahir* (apparent). But in respect of ownership it is classified into *al-mal al-ammah* (which has no specific owner) and *al-mal al-khassah* (which is owned by someone).

al-māl al-ʿain (المال العين)
Relating to the law of *zakat*, it is the definite property which has a bodily existence as opposed to *al dain*, the payment of which attaches a liability to a person as a result of a transaction or a loan or as damages for property destroyed.

al-māl al-bāṭin (المال الباطن)
Lit: Non-apparent wealth. *Tech*: That type of wealth which cannot be assessed or inspected by the *zakat* collector on the basis of any external evidence except that the owner chooses to disclose it. It includes, primarily, ornaments and cash holdings, etc.

al-māl al-ḍimār (المال الضمار)
Relating to the law of *zakat*, it is a property which has slipped out of one's hands with little chance of recovery, such as slaves lost, fugitive or gone astray; property fallen into sea or river; property usurped when there is no evidence to prove it. It also applies to all such property for which the owner despite possessing the title cannot derive benefit out of it or does not have actual possession or control of the property.

al-māl al-ghaib (المال الغيب)
Lit: Absent cash, capital not immediately available for use. *Tech*: Relating to the law of *mufawadah* partnership, no partnership can be valid with *al-mal al-ghaib*. *Al-mal al-hadir* (ready cash) is a necessary condition for a lawful partnership agreement.

al-māl al-ḥāḍir (المال الحاضر)
Lit: Ready cash. See *al-mal al-ghaib*.

māl al-jahbadhah (مال الجهبذة)
The commission or pay of the *jahbadh* for various functions performed by him. They were charged to the public (by collecting excessive taxes) or to the government by deducting from the tax proceeds.

al-māl al-kathīr (المال الكثير)

Lit: A large amount of wealth. *Tech*: The quantity of wealth on which *zakat* is levied.

al-māl al-mustafād (المال المستفاد)

Relating to the law of *zakat*, the property which was not in one's possession earlier but came into one's possession during the assessment year. Examples are monthly salary, wages, bonus, *gratis* receipts, etc. There is a controversy in the law about applicability of *zakat* on it.

al-māl al-mutaqawwam (المال المتقوم)

Wealth that has a commercial value. It is possible that certain wealth has no commercial value for Muslims (*ghair mutaqawwam*) but is valuable for non-muslims. Examples are wine and pork.

al-māl al-nāmī (المال النامي)

The wealth that increases by procreation or profit or has the potential to grow. Examples are livestock, cash, stock-in-trade and minerals.

māl al-qunyah (مال القنية)

Lit: Acquisition, property. *Tech*: Wealth which one holds for deriving benefits out of it rather than for trade.

al-māl al-ṣāmit (المال الصامت)

Relating to the law of *zakat*, it means goods lying dormant such as in the ownership of an orphan.

al-māl al-ẓāhir (المال الظاهر)

Lit: Apparent wealth. *Tech*: The type of wealth that can be inspected, examined and assessed by the *zakat* collector. Examples are livestock, agricultural produce, stock-in-trade and minerals.

al-ma'lūfah (المعلوفة)
Relating to the law of *zakat*, the cattle which are fed at the stable of the owner.

al-manīḥah (المنيحة)
Donation of a property with the permission to derive benefit from its yield without transferring the ownership to the donee. Examples are: donating a date-palm tree with permission to eat the fruit or donating a cow with permission to drink its milk. The property in question remains in the ownership of the donor. It is an important value of the Islamic economy.

al-manfa'ah (المنفعة)
Lit: Advantage, yield. *Tech*: Relating to the institution of *al-waqf*, it refers to the usufruct of the trust availed of by the beneficiaries. In case of *fai* lands which were a trust of the Muslims, the peasants were entitled to the *manafah* of the lands on the payment of rent (*kharaj*).

al-mann (المن)
A measure equivalent to two *ratl* Iraqi or 815.39 grams.

mannān (منان)
Lit: Beneficent, kind. *Tech*: Relating to *infaq*, one who recounts his charity and teases the recipient by it.

maqāṣid al-sharī'ah (مقاصد الشريعة)
Lit: Objectives of the *shariah*. *Tech*: It refers to the protection of life, religion, reason (*aql*), progeny and property. These objectives also define basic needs in an Islamic economy. See also *al-daruriyat al-khams*.

al-m'aqil (المعاقل)
Lit: Blood money. *Tech*: Mutual insurance 'societies' of pre-Islamic Arabia constituted to collect a common fund known as *al-kanz* to insure against damages and tort. If and when a member of the group committed a tort and had to pay damages, this

common fund came to his rescue. For instance, the damages for culpable homicide were one hundred camels. Few individuals could pay it. In such cases the *kanz* of the tribe was employed to pay for the damages. The members of the tribe were known as *aqilah*. The Prophet retained this practice. See *al-aqila*.

al-marḥalah (المرحلة)
A measure of distance equivalent to 2 *barid*, 8 *farasikh* or 44.352 kilometres.

mark-down
A financing technique adopted by commercial banks in Pakistan, applied, usually, for the encashment of bills of exchange. A person who needs short-term financing against a bill is provided finance after deducting a certain amount from the face value. The deduction is done at a fixed rate and is known as mark-down.

mark-up
A financing technique adopted by commercial banks in Pakistan. It is an agreement in which the bank agrees to finance the purchase of equipment or a commodity for its client at a price which includes a fixed pre-agreed profit for the bank.

al-maṣārif al-thamānīyah (المصارف الثمانية)
Eight heads of expenditure mentioned in the Quran about *zakat*, which are *fuqara*, *masakin*, *zakat*-collectors, those whose hearts have been reconciled, on freeing of slaves, debtors, *fi sabil* Allah (in the cause of Allah), and the wayfarers (Quran 9:60).

al-māshīyah (الماشيه)
Relating to the law of *zakat*, it refers to animal properties.

al-maslaḥah (المصلحة)
Lit: Utility, benefit. *Tech*: Exigencies which necessitate protection of faith, life, progeny, property and rationality. *Al-maslaḥah* is the basic consideration in the formulation of law in

Islam. Those acts or omissions which cause harm to the above named five *masalih* are known as *al-mafasid* and enactment against them becomes obligatory in the Islamic *shariah*.

Massraf Faisal al-Islami Bahamas (MFI/BAHAMAS)
Faisal Islamic Bank, Bahamas. Incorporated on 9 December 1982. A subsidiary of DMI. Began operations on 1 February 1984. Paid-up capital, US$2 million.

Massraf Faisal al-Islami of Bahrain (MFI/BAHRAIN)
Faisal Islamic Bank, Bahrain. A subsidiary of DMI. Incorporated on 14 July 1982. Authorized and paid-up capital, US$30 million.

al-matāʿ (المتاع)
It has a number of usages all of which are relevant for Islamic economics: enjoyment, object or delight, necessities of life, property, merchandise, household effects. The Quran refers to worldly possessions that are available for a very short span of time as compared to the pleasures of the Hereafter, which are everlasting. The Quran uses *al-mata* to denote insignificance of this world as compared to the life after death. (Quran 3:14, 3:185, 3:197, 4:77, 16:117).

al-mā ʿūn (الماعون)
Lit: Implement, utensil, instrument. *Tech*: Small household articles which neighbours or friends borrow from each other for temporary use without any consideration. Lending of *maun* is known as *ariyah* and has been recommended in the *shariah* as a virtuous act.

al-mauzūnāt (الموزونات)
Things which are ordinarily sold by measurement of weight, such as gold or silver. See also *al-makilat*.

al-mawāt (الموات)
See *al-ard al-mawat*.

maximum rate of profit

Relating to the *musharakah* financing by banks in Pakistan, it is the rate above which the banks cannot receive anything as their share of profit on the finance provided by them. It is determined in the following manner: (a) averaged-out rate of profits on PLS (Profit-Loss Sharing) longest term deposits paid by various banks. (b) Rate of service charges determined by the State Bank of Pakistan. Total of (a) and (b) above would be the maximum rate of profit.

al-maẓālim al-mushtarakah (المظالم المشتركة)

Tech: Extra-*shariah* taxes imposed on a group of people jointly. This practice has been disapproved by jurists.

al-mil (الميل)

Lit: Mile. *Tech*: It is equal to 4000 *dhira*, one mile plus 240 yards or 1,848 meters.

al-milk (الملك)

Expression of the connection between a man and a thing which is under one's absolute power and control to the exclusion of control and disposition by others. But the *milk* of individuals or society is regulated by the *shariah* since absolute *milk* belongs to God.

al-milk al-ʿāmmah (الملك العامة)

Public property such as roads and large waterways. They are also called *ghair mamluk* (not owned), and can be used by an individual so far as it does not involve navigation or the use does not deprive the shareholders of their water supply. Likewise, roads must not be blocked by the erection of buildings.

al-milk al-tāmm (الملك التام)

Lit: Perfect ownership. *Tech*: Complete and total ownership of an asset.

minimum rate of profit

Relating to the *musharakah* financing by bankers in Pakistan, it is the rate below which no financing is provided by the banks, arrived at in the following manner: (a) Averaged-out rate of profit paid on PLS (profit-loss sharing) saving accounts by various banks. (b) Rate of service charges determined by the State Bank of Pakistan. Total of (a) and (b) would be the minimum rate of profit.

mīrī ʾarāḍī (میری اراضی)
Kharaj lands in the Ottoman empire. Also known as *amiri aradi*, i.e., lands belonging to the *amir*.

al-misāḥah (المساحة)
Lit: Measuring or surveying land, taxing for unit of area. *Tech*: During the Muslim period, one of the bases for land taxation used to be *ala al-misahah*, that is, tax calculated on the amount of land tilled, keeping in mind the location and fertility of the soil. The term was used to express two related meanings. First, tax assessed on the basis of measurements of land independent of any fluctuations in the area tilled or crop produced, assessed for the lunar year and paid, quite frequently, in monthly instalments. Second, land-tax assessed on the basis of area sown, leaving out fallow and waste land, assessing different rates for different crops, for the solar year.

al-miskīn (المسكين)
Used in the law of *zakat* for a person who has been rendered helpless or invalid by sickness, old age or war and is either unable to work or can not earn enough to maintain himself and his family.

al-mithlī (المثلى)
Lit: Fungibles. *Tech*: Muslim jurists have distinguished between things that are distinguishable and those that are indistinguishable. For example, different units of wheat, corn or grapes are not distinguishable. If a person borrows 1 kilogram of wheat, he must return 1 kilogram of wheat, but it is not possible precisely to distinguish between the wheat borrowed and the wheat

returned. The two are indistinguishable, or *mithli*. See *al-qimi* for distinguishable things.

al-mithqāl (المثقال)

A weight for measuring commodities, equivalent to 4.5 grams.

al-mithqāl bi dhahab (المثقال بالذهب)

A weight to measure gold, equivalent to 4.25 grams.

money muḍārabah

A contract of *mudarabah* in which the capital owner provides capital in cash (*ain*).

al-mu'ājarah (المواجرة)

A contract in which a landlord leases his land to a tenant for a fixed sum of money or anything else usually paid in advance.

al-mu'ākarah (المواكرة)

An alternate term for *al-muajarah*.

mu'allafatul qulūb (مؤلفة القلوب)

Lit: Those whose hearts have been reconciled. *Tech*: Used in the context of *zakat*, one of the eight heads of accounts on which it can be spent. In the days of the Prophet, the *zakat* fund was also expended on those who could be a potential danger to Islam, who have been converted to Islam and needed economic support or who could go back to *kufr* if not supported. All schools of jurisprudence agree that this head of account is still alive and the Islamic state can appropriate *zakat* for it. Those who receive *zakat* on this account can be Muslims or non-Muslims, rich or poor, nationals or aliens.

al-mu'āmalah (المعاملة)

Lit: Economic transaction. *Tech*: Lease of land or of fruit trees for money, in kind or for a share of the crop.

al-muʿāmalah fi al-thimār (المعاملة فى الثمار)

A tenure in which the orchard owner gives his fruit trees to a worker who irrigates the soil with buckets, by water-wheel or in some other way; fecundates the trees; and fulfills all the requirements of tillage until the time when the fruit becomes sound enough to be sold. In exchange, the worker gets one-half, one-third or one-fourth of the fruit.

al-muʿāwamah (المعاومة)

Selling the fruit on trees for a period of one, two or three years, even before the fruit has appeared.

al-mubādharah (المباذرة)

Agricultural contract in which seeds and other things are provided by the landlord and the tenant receives a mere sixth or seventh part of the produce.

mubāh ʾumūmī (مباح عمومى)

Things and advantages which are open to everyone and cannot be exclusively appropriated by anyone. Examples are air, light, fire, grass, seawater, rivers, streams, public roads and grazing fields for the cattle.

al-muḍārabah (المضاربة)

A form of business contract in which one party brings capital and the other personal effort. The proportionate share in profit is determined by mutual consent. But the loss is borne only by the owner of the capital, in which case the entrepreneur gets nothing for his labour. The financier is known as *rabb al-mal* and the worker or entrepreneur as *mudarib*. As a financing technique adopted by Islamic banks, it is a contract in which all the capital is provided by the Islamic bank while the business is managed by the other party. The profit is shared in pre-agreed ratios, and loss, if any, unless caused by the negligence or violation of the terms of the contract by the *mudarib*, is borne by the Islamic bank. The bank passes on this loss to the depositers.

muḍārabah market
See *qirad market*.

muḍārabah certificate
A financial instrument devised by Islamic investment companies to mobilize funds for investment. A *mudarabah* certificate can be for a specific purpose or for a general purpose. The former is related to financing of specific projects and matures only on the completion of the project. The latter can have a specific or indefinite duration. Both the types can be issued in negotiable form either registered or to the bearer. The *mudarabah* certificates can be distributed in an underwriting or sales effort for a fixed term or can be continuously available or be available on a periodic basis.

al-muḍārabah al-muṭlaqah (المضاربة المطلقة)
Lit: Unconditional *mudarabah*. *Tech*: A *mudarabah* which does not bind the enterpreneur about the place, time, season, commodities, credit or techniques of trade. These matters are left to the option of the enterpreneur. The *mudarabah* contract defines merely the profit-sharing ratio.

al-muḍārabah al-muqayyadah (المضاربة المقيدة)
Lit: Conditional *mudarabah*. *Tech*: A contract of *mudarabah* in which certain conditions like place, season, commodities, credit and techniques of trade are stipulated by the *rabb al-mal*.

muḍārabah shares
Normally issued by the state, they are an instrument for obtaining funds from the private sector on the basis of *mudarabah*. The state issues a share certificate, indicating the price, the period and the terms of the contract. The funds thus collected can be invested in the profit-yielding projects so that the state can share profit or loss with the public.

al-muḍārib (المضارب)
In a *mudarabah* contract, the person who acts as enterpreneur. See also *sahib al-mal* and *rabb al-mal*.

al-mudd **(المد)**

Lit: A weight or measure. *Tech*: According to Hanafites it is equivalent to two *ratl*, 1.032 litres or 815.39 grams. According to other jurists it is equivalent to 1–⅓ *ratl*, 0.687 litres or 543 grams.

al-muddakhar **(المدخر)**

Lit: Something which can be stored. *Tech*: Relating to *riba al-fadl*, the Malikites apply the concept of *riba al-fadl* to items which are both *muqtat* (quality of being a food item) and *muddakhar* (storable).

al-mufāwaḍah **(المفاوضة)**

See *shirkah al-mufawadah*.

al-mughārasah **(المغارسة)**

Lit: A contract for planting trees. *Tech*: A contract in which a landlord gives his bare land to a worker to plant fruit trees. It may be done in two lawful ways: first, the landlord bears all expenses of transplantation of twigs, fixtures, of date stones and pruning of branches and twigs; he hires a worker/tenant to plant the tree and to work and irrigate it for a certain fixed period until the plant yields fruit—in exchange for this work, he gets fixed, definitely known wages or a certain piece of that land, i.e., he becomes co-owner of the trees. Second, the tenant is made responsible for all these expenses including plantation of the fruit trees, its mending, irrigation, etc., and in exchange he obtains a certain stipulated share—one half, one third, one fourth, or more or less of the fruit crop. In that case the worker can have no right over the land. The period for this tenancy is not fixed and all other terms and conditions of the contract of *muzara'a* apply in this tenure. This term is used by Ibn Hazm.

al-muḥāqalah **(المحاقلة)**

It denotes a deal involving lease of land against corn and/or buying of a crop still in growth when grains are in the ears in exchange for corn.

al-muḥtajir (المحتجر)
One who fences a dead land for the purpose of developing it.

al-muhtakir (المحتكر)
One who stockholds commodities (especially foodgrains) with the intention of causing a shortage in the market and pushing up the price.

al-muḥtasib (المحتسب)
Head of *al-hisba* department during the Muslim reign. His main responsibilities were (a) enforcing the proper behaviour (*maruf*) and preventing the improper (*munkar*), (b) supervision of markets, (c) helping the state in keeping the flows of supply and demand unobstructed. He had wide executive and juridical powers. The *muhtasib* was often a scholar of the *shariah*.

al-mujāmalah (المجاملة)
Lit: Mutual kindness. *Tech*: Informal partnership prevalent during Fatimade and Ayubide Egypt.

al-mukātab (المكاتب)
The slave who obtained from his master the privilege of manumission on payment of a fixed price. Such slaves had the right to engage in trade and buy and sell in order to earn the price of their freedom but they did not own goods completely.

al-mukhābarah (المخابرة)
An agreement to lease land on rent for cultivation with the condition to share the produce in a given ratio. In some cases the agreement provides for the supply of seed by the landowner but it is not always the essence of the contract.

al-mukhāḍarah (المخاضرة)
Sale of fruit or crop before it has ripened.

al-mukhammin (المخمن)
A valuer for estimating crops when still on the root, employed by the tax departments during the Abbaside period.

al-mukhāṭarah (المخاطرة)
A wagering contract or a risky contract. It applies to all those contracts which may bring a reward without any human effort or to contracts which involve non-business risks.

al-mulamasah (الملامسه)
See *bai al-mulamasah*.

al-muljam (الملجم)
A measure equivalent to 2.5 *sa*. According to Hanafites one *muljam* is equal to 8.154 kilograms or 8.425 litres, while other jurists consider it equal to 5.43 kilograms or 6.87 litres.

mulk lands
Ushri lands in the Ottoman empire.

multipurpose muḍārabah
A *mudarabah* contract which has more than one specific purpose or objective.

al-munābadhah (المنابذة)
See *bai al-munabadhah*.

al-muqāraḍah (المقارضه)
An agreement in which a person leaves his commodities (stock-in-trade) with another person so that the latter may sell them. The profit is for the owner of the commodities. Also used as an alternate term for *mudarabah*.

al-muqāriḍ (المقارض)
In a contract of *mudarabah*, one who furnishes the funds. Also termed as *rabb al-mal*.

al-muqāsamah (المقاسمة)
Lit: Partnership. *Tech*: A contract of partnership to till land for sharing the produce. The classical example is that of the Prophet's contract with the Jews of Khaiber. He agreed to share

the produce of the land with the Jews, retaining them as tillers of the land.

al-muqāṣṣah (المقاصة)

Lit: Accounting, clearing, settlement of accounts. *Tech*: Used in *riba*-free banking. The operation of current account deposits is governed by the juridical principle of *muqassah*, which denotes that the original deposit was a loan to the bank and its drawal is a loan of the bank to depositor. Both the loans cancel each other (*muqassah*).

al-muqāṭa'ah (المقاطعة)

A system of taxation followed by Umayyads and Abbasides. It referred to a procedure for unlimited collective tax payment which was payable by a few persons and constituted income for the state and the caliph. It was used in a number of ways: (a) a fixed yearly sum of money payable according to agreement and without regard to the prosperity of the cultivator or the population; (b) an annual due paid for a fief; (c) a tax paid by allied nations and provinces as a tribute on condition of retaining a certain autonomy; (d) dues paid by the one who undertakes the tax management of an entire province or a major area. In the Ottoman empire the system was classified into three categories: *Timar*, *Emanet* and *Iltizam*. The first form was similar to the fief system of European feudalism, whereby the feudal lord kept the income and in return was obliged to perform certain services for the state. The second form constituted income from properties administered on a trustee basis, which was handed over to the state in return for a reward. The third form was tax tenure whereby the tax tenant (*amin*) was allowed to keep a part of the taxes for himself and had to give the rest to the state.

al-muqāyaḍah (المقايضة)

See *bai al-muqayadah*.

al-muqtāt

Something which has the quality of becoming a food item.

Relating to *riba al-fadl*, the *Shafiites* apply the above concept to food items (*al-muqtat*) only.

al-murābaḥah (المرابحة)
See *bai al-murabahah*.

al-murāhanah (المراهنة)
Bet by two parties on the happening of an event in the future so that one will pay the other a certain amount if the event takes place; otherwise, the latter will pay the former. This is a form of gambling.

al-murāṭalah (المراطلة)
Selling by counterpoising gold for gold or dirhams for dirhams.

al-murū'ah (المرؤة)
Lit: Manliness, valour, sense of honour, generosity. *Tech*: Spending on the hospitality, honour and gifts of the well-to-do and respectable people. This is in contrast to *sadaqah*, which is meant for the poor and the needy.

al-murūj (المروج)
A category of common land (*hima*) in early Arabic society where cattle could graze. The village owned it collectively so that its residents could sell or develop it as an owner of a private property. It was possible to parcel it out to single members of the community who might cultivate it.

al-musabbab (المسبب)
Taxes assigned to certain claimants or provinces as against *mahmul*, taxes collected from provinces and carried to the central treasury.

al-muṣādarah (المصادرة)
Confiscation of property by the state without compensation.

al-musāqah **(المساقاة)**

A contract in which the owner of the garden shares its produce with another person in a pre-determined ratio in return for latter's services in irrigating the garden.

al-muṣarrah **(المصيرة)**

Lit: The animal which is not milked and its milk is left in the udders. *Tech*: Used in a sales contract whereby the seller of milk cattle keeps the cattle un-milked for a day or so and deceives the buyer by milking a larger quantity in his presence than is usual for the cattle.

al-musāwamah **(المساومة)**

See *bai al-musawamah*.

al-musinnah **(المسنة)**

Relating to the *nisab* of *zakat*, a cow in her third year. This is also used for two-year-old sheep and goats.

al-mushārakah **(المشاركة)**

A financing technique adopted by Islamic banks. It is an agreement under which the Islamic bank provides funds which are mingled with the funds of the business enterprise and others. All providers of capital are entitled to participate in management, but not necessarily required to do so. The profit is distributed among the partners in pre-agreed ratios, while the loss is borne by each partner strictly in proportion to respective capital contributions.

al-mushāʿ **(المشاع)**

Lit: Common; undivided. *Tech*: Mixing up of the proprietary rights of more than one person in a thing, such as in joint ownership where each co-owner has a right until all particles of the property are divided.

al-musharrif **(المشرف)**

Tax-collector in fourteenth century Muslim Spain. He used to be responsible to one of the secretaries (*katibs*) of the sultan called *sahib al-ashghal*.

mushrif (مشرف)
Relating to the administration of *iqta* in sixteenth century India, the *mushrif* was a treasury officer who authenticated accounts and other writings.

al-mustaḍʿafīn (المستضعفين)
See *al-mustakbirin*.

al-mustakbirīn (المستكبرين)
Quranic term for 'haves' in the society. The Quran comments on the unjust distribution of economic power which results in the emergence of two distinct classes in the society: *al-mustakbirin* and *al-mustadafin*. The former are economically powerful and corrupt people who oppress the weaker sections of society. The latter consist of economically weak and oppressed people who remain contented with their fate.

al-mustakhrij (المستخرج)
In Abbaside Iraq, an official of the tax department who worked for the *jahbadh*.

al-mustarsil (المسترسل)
Lit: Loose, flowing (hair), friendly, affable. *Tech*: A buyer who does not haggle over the price; also a buyer who is unaware of the actual price of a commodity and is willing to buy at the price quoted by the seller. Some jurists have also included in this category those farmers who bring their produce to the market but, being unaware of the market conditions, sell their produce at a price lower than the prevailing rate.

mustawfī (مستوفى)
See *diwan al-mal*.

mutaqabbil
One who undertakes the contract of *qabalah* or tax-farming, in which a contractor pays the ruler an agreed amount, collects taxes from the people and retains the difference. In modern parlance, it was privatization of tax collection, a tyrannical system. See *al-qabalah*.

al-muwaṣalah (المواصلة)
Lit: Close relationship. *Tech*: Informal partnership during Fatimide and Ayubide Egypt.

al-muzābanah (المزابنة)
See *bai al-muzabanah*.

al-muzār'ah (المزارعة)
It is a contract in which one person agrees to till the land of the other person in consideration for a part of the produce of the land.

N

al-nafal (pl. al-anafāl) (النفل)
Lit: Booty, spoil. *Tech*: In a broad sense it covers the *ghanimah* and the *fai*, but in its narrower sense it is a share of the booty given to the warrior for performing an excellent job on the battlefield. It is additional to his regular share in the booty that is given for specific duties on the battlefield.

al-najash (النجش)
See *al-tanajush*.

al-nājiz (الناجز)
Lit: Entire, complete. *Tech*: Relating to the commercial law, it refers to a transaction for ready cash.

al-naqd (النقد)
Gold and silver in the form of coins.

al-naqdain (النقدين)
Lit: Two currencies. *Tech*: Gold and silver or dinar and dirham used as currencies. Also called *al-nuqud*.

al-naql (النقل)
Transfer or transportation of a property from one place to another with the intention of giving the possession to the other party.

al-naqqal (النقال)
A person employed to transport or carry the goods collected as *zakat*. He is included in the category of *amilin* and is paid out of the *zakat* funds.

al-nashsh (النش)
Lit: Half of anything. *Tech*: A weight equivalent to half *uqiyah*, 20 dirhams or 59.5 grams.

naṣīb al-mithl (نصيب المثل)
Lit: Similar share. *Tech*: In relation to an agreement of partnership, such as *shirkah*, *mudarabah*, *muzarah*, *musaqah*, etc., it is the share of the parties to agreement in the profit, in case the original agreement turns *fasid* for any reason. In such cases each one is given *nasib al-mithl*: the familiar share or the share which is known and acceptable in similar cases in the society.

al-nāʿūrah (الناعورة)
See *al-dālīyah*.

al-nawāḍih (النواضح)
Relating to the law of *zakat*, it refers to camels which irrigate land. Half-*ushr* is usually payable on the produce of the land worked by *al-nawadih*.

al-nawāh (النواة)
Lit: Date pit, stone of a date. *Tech*: A weight equivalent to 5 dirhams or 14.875 grams.

al-nawā'ib **(النوائب)**

Lit: Calamity, misfortune. *Tech*: Those taxes which are imposed to meet any emergency due to some misfortune or natural calamity. Also used for irregular levies of Muslim states imposed collectively on the people anywhere. Jurists opposed these levies, but they were in vogue during mediaeval Islam.

nāẓir al-awqaf **(ناظر الاوقاف)**

Administrator of an endowment or trust.

nāẓir al-sikkah **(ناظر السكة)**

A fourteenth century Spanish institution. The *nazir al-sikkah* was an officer in the mint responsible for supervising the quality of the coins minted. This office was usually filled by jurists.

nāẓir al-sūq **(ناظر السوق)**

An alternate term for *al-muhtasib* prevalent in North Africa during the third century of hijra. See *al-muhtasib*.

al-nāzirah **(الناظرة)**

Postponement of debt at the request of the debtor who is facing difficulty in repayment at the due date. Along with *qard hasan*, it is an important element of the *riba*-free credit structure.

al-niṣāb **(النصاب)**

Exemption limit for the payment of *zakat*. It is different for different types of wealth.

niẓām al-misaḥah **(نظام المساحة)**

Relating to the administration of land revenue, the system of levying *kharaj* on the basis of area cultivated irrespective of the produce. This system remained in vogue from the times of the first four caliphs to the times of the Abbaside caliph Mehdi who changed it to *nizam al-muqasamah*, i.e., the system of tax on the basis of the produce.

niẓām al-muqāsamah **(نظام المقاسمة)**
Relating to the administration of land revenue, the system of levying *kharaj* on the basis of the produce of land. This was adopted by the Abbaside caliph Mehdi. The system of land revenue on *ushri* lands was also that of *muqasmah*.

P

partnership shares
Proposed in the model of interest-free banking by some. Normally to be issued by the state, they are an instrument for obtaining funds from the private sector for investment in the public sector on the basis of partnership. The holders of these share certificates are the owners of the respective enterprises in which their funds have been invested. These shares are transferable and marketable.

PLS counters
Profit-loss sharing counters opened from 1 January 1980 at the five nationalized banks of Pakistan. The counters accepted deposits for varying duration and used them for financing on the basis of *al-musharkah*, *al-mudarabah*, *bai al-muajjal* and *bai al-murabahah*.

PLS ratio
Profit-loss sharing ratio used in the interest-free banking model of the Council of Islamic Ideology, Pakistan (1980). The PLS ration is the ratio of financiers' funds with the entrepreneurs' funds. It has been suggested as a monetary tool in lieu of the interest-based bank rate.

PLS system
Profit-loss sharing system proposed by the Panel of Economists and Bankers and endorsed by the Council of Islamic Ideology, Pakistan (1980). The PLS system is the main plank of Islamization of banks in Pakistan. Under the system the savers deposit

their funds on the basis of profit-loss sharing. The banks provide finance on the basis of approved modes such as *musharakah*, *mudarabah*, mark-up, mark-down, leasing, lease-purchase and rent-sharing.

productive muḍarabah
A contract of *mudarabah* wherein the owner of a commodity/raw material gives the material to an artisan/worker to manufacture a certain product with the stipulation that the finished product will be sold and the profit will be shared by them.

profit-sharing certificates (PSC)
A proposed instrument of *riba*-free banking. The certificate would be offered by commercial banks to savers. A profit-sharing certificate involves investing a certain sum of money into short term operations. Its maturity can vary from sixty days to one year. It offers diversification among short-term placements. All these characteristics would make it especially marketable and relatively attractive to savers who desire to stay closer to the higher edge of the liquidity spectrum

profit-sharing deposits
Financial instrument of *riba*-free economy. Indicates deposits with commercial banks on the basis of profit sharing.

provisional rate of profit
Relating to the *musharakah* financing by banks in Pakistan, it means the rate which is determined after deducting a good management fee from the projected rate of profit and after taking into account the weightage, if any, given to any of the funds deployed. See *good management fee*.

PSC
See *profit-sharing certificates*.

PSD
See *profit-sharing deposits*.

PTC

Participation Term Certificate, a financing instrument used by Islamized banks in Pakistan to replace debentures. Holders of the PTC share in the profit or loss of companies raising finance. Usually issued for a maximum period of ten years, secured by a charge on the assets of the company, the PTCs have a prior claim on the profits of the company. Any loss is first met from past reserves, and any left-over loss is shared by all providers of the capital including PTC holders. In practice, PTC has imbibed the spirit of interest. The PTC scheme requires a 'pre-production discount rate' on long-gestation period projects. Similarly, when the company does not have profits to pay to holders of PTCs, then it is required to issue additional PTCs in the name of existing holders, the amount being equal to the expected profit of the PTC holders. In certain cases, the PTC holders may also get equity holdings equal to the loss of the company. The PTC holder does not suffer a loss in any case. Thus the PTC is against the Islamic principles of trade and is more akin to *riba*.

Q

al-qabālah (القبالة)

Used in two senses. First, it is equivalent to that form of tenancy in which the landlord receives a fixed share of the crop or a fixed sum of money or both; it is thus almost synonymous with *muzarah* and *kira al-ard*. Second, tax-farming in which a tax-farmer guarantees and pays a lump sum to the state and obtains the right to collect rents and revenues from the contract land, retaining the difference between the two.

al-qabil (القبيل)

In a contract of *qabalah*, a person who provides surety in landed property for the payment of tax. It is used in the same sense as *al-kafil*. The *qabil* was a tax-farmer who acted as an intermediary between the tax payers and the government's tax collectors.

When a person entered into a contract of *qabalah*, he was assumed to be accountable for a fair treatment of the tax payers besides being responsible for such development works as levelling of land, water-supply channels and rural roads. His expenses for this were met by *diwan al-kharaj*. The contract of *qabalah* was awarded by public auction. The tax farmers were usually local chiefs, ex-administrative officers, managers and merchants. The contract was given to the lowest bidder. The bid meant the wage the tax farmer would claim for collecting and depositing the tax (which was often in kind).

al-qafīz (القفيز)
Lit: A dry measure. *Tech*: One *qafiz* is equal to 12 *sa*. According to Hanafites it is equal to 39.138 kilograms or 40.344 litres, while according to other jurists it is equal to 26.064 kilograms or 32.974 litres.

al-qafīz al-ḥajjājī (القفيز الحجاجى)
A grain measure, one *qafiz hajjaji*: 8 *ratls*, 96 *uqiyah*, 12343.68 *dirhams* or 3.262 kilograms.

qafīz al-ṭaḥḥān (قفيز الطحان)
Lit: A measure of flour given to the grinder of grains as wage for his services. *Tech*: Basis of the Hanafite law that no wages should be paid in the form of the product produced by the labourer.

al-qanā'ah (القناعة)
Lit: Contentment; frugality. *Tech*: Attitude of a Muslim to remain contented with what he gets after struggle in a lawful manner.

al-qānūn (القانون)
Lit: Law. *Tech*: Abbreviated from *qanun al kharaj*, the rent roll that was the basis of the tax levy.

al-qarḍ (القرض)
Lit: To cut, to sever. *Tech*: Loan of *mithli* articles (such as money)

with the stipulation to return its like in the future. It is a general term for monetary loans without a deadline to return it.

al-qarḍ al hasan (القرض الحسن)
Lit: A virtuous loan. *Tech*: A loan with the stipulation to return the principal sum in the future without any increase.

al-qaṣabah (القصبة)
A measure of length: 13.6604 square metres.

al-qassām (القسام)
Tech: Relating to *zakat* administration, it refers to the person appointed to distribute *zakat* revenues.

al-qaṭaʿ (القطع)
See *al-muqataah*.

al-qaṭāīʿ (sing: *al-qatīʿah*) (القطاعى)
See *al-iqta*.

Qatar Islamic Bank (QIB)
Incorporated on 7 July 1983. Authorized capital, QR200 million. Paid-up capital, QR50 million.

al-qīmah (القيمة)
Lit: Value, worth, size of an amount. *Tech*: Price of an article as prevalent in the market as compared to *thaman* which is the price of an article as agreed by the buyer and the seller irrespective of the marker price.

al-qimār (القمار)
Lit: Gambling. *Tech*: An agreement in which possession of a property is contingent upon the happening of an uncertain event. By implication it applies to those agreements in which there is a definite loss for one party and definite gain for the other without specifying which party will lose and which will gain.

al-qīmī (القيمى)

Lit: Non-fungibles. *Tech*: Things that are distinguishable. For example, if a person borrows a horse, it is not the same thing to return any horse. Horses are distinguishable by colour, age, lineage, etc., and are therefore *qimi*. See *al-mithli* for indistinguishable things.

al-qinṭār (القنطار)

A weight of varying measures in different periods of Muslim history. It refers to a large quantity of gold and silver. Some say it was equal to 1200 *uqiyah*; others say it was equal to 1000 *dinars*; still other's think it was equal to 1200 *dirhams*. In another opinion it was 80,000 *dirhams* or 100 *ratl* of gold.

al-qirāḍ (القراض)

An alternate term for *al-mudarabah*.

qirāḍ market

Market for *qirad* funds. In Islamic economy funds for *qirad* may be available through banks, insurance companies, joint stock companies, mutual funds, investment trusts and other financial intermediaries. The supply of and demand for *qirad* funds determines the ratio for distributing uncertain outcomes of the enterprise. This ratio has been variously termed in the literature as *qirad* rate, profit-share, B.R.P-D.R.P., *mudarabah* rate, etc. The *qirad* market automatically adjusts this rate but the central bank may also intervene and prescribe *qirad* rates for different sectors.

al-qīraṭ (القيراط)

A measure of weight and length of varying sizes in different ages. A *qirat* for measuring silver and commodities is equivalent to 0.248 grams and for measuring gold, 0.2120 grams. For measuring length, a *qirat* is equivalent to 175 metres.

al-qirbah (القربة)

Lit: A skin bag for water. *Tech*: A measure for liquids equivalents to 40 *sa* or 68.48 litres.

qismatul ghuramā' (قسمة الغرماء)
Distribution of the assets of the bankrupt among the creditors in proportion to their debts.

al-qisṭ (القسط)
Lit: A measure. *Tech*: One qist is 0.5 *sa*. According to Hanafites it is equal to 1.631 kilograms or 1.680 litres, while according to other jurists it is equal to 1.086 kilograms or 1.374 litres.

al-qiyās (القياس)
Lit: Measure, example, comparison, analogy. *Tech*: Derivation of the law on the analogy of another law if the basis (*'illah*) of the two is the same. It is a primary source of Islamic economics.

al-Qur'ān (القرآن)
The book of Allah revealed to the Prophet Muhammad and transmitted to the present age through an incessant chain.

al-quṣārah (القصارة)
In a contract of *muhaqalah*, grains left over in the ears after thrashing. The *qusarah* also belonged to the landlord.

R

al-rabā'yah (الرباعيه)
Relating to the *nisab* of *zakat*, a she-camel in her seventh year.

Rabb (رب)
Attribute of God as the sustainer of the entire universe. Sustenance includes fostering, bringing up, regulating and completing the evolution of things from the crudest state to that of the highest perfection. God is *Rabb* of the entire universe. Belief in Him as a sustainer is basic to Islam and defines a large number of socio-economic relations in a Muslim society.

rabb al-'arḍ (رب الأرض)
Landlord in a contract of *muzarah*.

rabb al-'aṣl (رب الأصل)
Owner of capital in a contract of *mudarabah*.

rabb al-māl (رب المال)
In a *mudarabah* contract, the person who invests the capital.

rabb al-salam (رب السلم)
A buyer in a contract of *bai al-salam*.

al-rabī' (الربيع)
Streamlet for irrigation of land. Regarding contract of *muzarah* in pre-Islamic days, the crop grown on the area irrigated by the *rabi* was considered to be the share of the landlord.

al-raḍkh (pl. al-arḍākh). (الرضخ)
Lit: A small, paltry gift. *Tech*: A small gift from out of *ghanimah* for non-combatants (*ghair ghanimin*).

al-rafāh (الرفاه)
Enjoyment of comforts and amenities with humility and obedience to God. See *Taraf*.

al-rahn (الرهن)
Lit: Pledge or pawn. *Tech*: Placing a property under detention and suspension in consideration of a right against its owner to be satisfied out of that property. Also known as *al-rahn al-maqbudah*.

al-rahn bil darak (الرهن بالدرك
For the buyer to keep something as mortgage in case of a third party's later claim on the goods; withholding a part of the price as a mortgage.

al-Rajhi Company for Islamic Investment Saudi Arabia
Incorporated in December 1980. Has 230 branches in Saudi Arabia.

al-rashā' (الرشاد)
See *al-gharb*.

rate of muḍārabah
Ratio of profit-sharing between the owner of the capital and the entrepreneur, who uses these funds on the basis of *mudarabah*. It is an alternative for or parallel to the rate of interest in the capitalist economy where funds are advanced by one party to the other as a loan. Manipulation in the rate of *mudarabah* can be made to adjust the supply of and demand for investible funds in the Islamic economy.

raṭl bil-'ashyā' (رطل بالأشياء)
Lit: A weight. *Tech*: One *ratl* is 128.57 *dirhams* or 407.695 grams.

raṭl al-fiḍḍah (رطل الفضة)
A weight equal to 480 *dirhams*, 12 *'uqiyah* or 1428.4 grams.

rent-sharing
A mode of financing adopted by financial institutions in Pakistan, according to which the financial institution provides part of the finance for construction of a house. The client and the financial institution share in the presumptive rent of the house. Since maintenance and taxes are to be paid by the client, a suitable allowance is given to him in the share of the rent. Similarly, the financial institution's share is adjusted upward to provide for administrative expenses. But all legal charges are paid by the client and the house remains mortgaged until the financial institution receives back all due to it.

al-ribā (الربا)
Lit: An excess or increase. *Tech*: An increase which in a loan transaction or in exchange of a commodity accrues to the owner (lender) without giving an equivalent counter-value or recompense (*'iwad*) in return to the other party; every increase which is without an *'iwad* or equal counter-value.

ribā al-'ajlān (ربا العجلان)
An alternate term for *riba al-fadl*: the *riba* which accrues to the money-lender immediately, as in a contract of barter sale. This

is in contrast to *riba al-nasiah* where, the *riba* accrues after the passage of a term.

ribā al-buyū' (ربا البيوع)
An alternate term for *riba al-fadl*.

ribā al-duyūn (ربا الديون)
A substitute expression for the Quranic *riba* or *riba al-nasiah*.

ribā al-faḍl (ربا الفضل)
A sale transaction of the *amwal al-ribawiyyah* (those commodities in which the injuction of *riba* is applicable) in which a commodity is exchanged for the same commodity but unequal in amount and the delivery of at least one commodity is postponed. To avoid *riba al-fadl*, the exchange of commodities from both sides should be equal and instant (*yadan bi yadin*). *Riba al-fadl* has been prohibited by the Prophet as a measure to forestall the *riba* from creeping into the economy through the back door.

ribā al-jāhiliyyah (ربا الجاهلية)
The *riba* prevalent in Arabia in pre-Islamic days.

ribā al-jalī (ربا الجلى)
Lit: Manifest increment. *Tech*: An alternate term for *riba al-Quran*.

ribā al-khafī (ربا الخفى)
Lit: Concealed increment. An alternate term for *riba al-fadl*.

ribā al-nasī'ah (ربا النسيئة)
Increment on the principal of a loan payable by the borrower. It refers to the practice of lending money for any length of time on the understanding that the borrower would return to the lender at the end of this period the amount originally lent together with an increment in consideration of the lender having granted him time to pay. The increment was known as *riba al-nasiah*. It was in vogue in Arabia in the days of the Prophet.

ribā al-Qur'ān (ربا القرآن)
The *riba* which has been explicitly prohibited in the Quran. See *riba al-sunna*.

ribā al-sunnah (ربا السنة)
Riba-borne dealings, prevalent in Arabia of the Prophet, prohibited by the *sunnah* of the Prophet. An alternate term for *riba al-fadl*. See *Riba al-Quran*.

ribā al-yad (ربا اليد)
A sale transaction which involves barter exchange of the same commodity in unequal amounts and postponed delivery by either or both parties. An alternate term for *riba al-fadl*.

al-rībah (ريبه)
Lit: Doubtful. *Tech*: Income which has the semblance of *riba* or which raises doubts about its legality.

al-ribḥ al-mu'tād (ربح المعتاد)
Lit: Usual profit, normal profit. *Tech*: The rate of profit prevalent in a trade in a competitive market. Although there is no quantitative limit on the rate of profit in the shariah, it is not expected to go beyond *al-ribh al-mutad*. Charging profit over and above this is condemned in a Muslim society.

al-rikāz (الركاز)
Hidden treasure.

al-riqāb (الرقاب)
Lit: To liberate a soul. *Tech*: One of the eight heads of account mentioned in the Quran on which *zakat* can be appropriated, meaning to spend money for the liberation of slaves. These days this head of account does not seem to be relevant.

risk exposure factor (r.e.f)
In relation to *riba*-free banking, it has been argued by some people that weight should be given to capital in proportion to its

exposure to risk and period of investment before sharing profit or loss, which is the risk exposure factor. Capital at face value is to be multiplied by the r.e.f. for arriving at the *effective capital*, which see.

al-rizq (الرزق)
Lit: Livelihood, means of living, subsistence. *Tech*: It has been used to denote all the resources at the disposal of man on this earth. God speaks of these resources as one of His blessings. Man is accountable to God for his *rizq*, whereas God has assumed it as His responsibility to provide means of sustenance to all animate beings.

al-ruqʿah (الرقعة)
Banking instrument of the mediaeval Muslim period. It was a payment order to draw money from the bank.

ruqʿah al-ṣairif (رقعة الصيرف)
Lit: Paper slip of the money-changer. *Tech*: A type of promissory note prevalent in the twelfth century A.D. Muslim world to facilitate retail and wholesale commercial transactions. It was issued by bankers to individual merchants who had actually made payments to the banks, who had money or valuable goods deposited in the bank or who simply were preferred customers.

al-ruqbā (الرقبى)
Tech: Giving a property to someone on the condition that if the donor dies before the donee it shall become the property of the donee and his heirs but if the donee dies first the property given shall return to the donor.

al-rushd (الرشد)
Lit: Good conduct, sensible conduct. *Tech*: Prudence in the utilization of one's property. *Al-rushd* is an essential condition for the right to own property in Islam.

S

al-ṣāʿ (الصاع)

Lit: A cubic measure of varying magnitude. *Tech*: One *sa* equals 8 *ratl* (in Hanafite school) or 5.33 *ratl* in other schools. In Hanafite school it is equivalent to 3.2615 kg, whereas in other schools it is equivalent to 2.172 kg. For measuring liquids, it is equal to 3.363 litres according to Hanafites and 2.748 litres according to others.

al-ṣabr (الصبر)

Lit: Patience. *Tech*: A value of Islamic society. Muslims are enjoined to bear economic hardship with patience and not to feel inclined towards acquiring resources by unlawful means. It does not preclude, however, protest against economic injustice and exploitation.

al-ṣadaqah (الصدقة)

Lit: Charity. *Tech*: In its widest sense it means an attitude of mutual appreciation, affection, mutual assistance, an act of loyalty to God and to one's fellow beings, a sense of true humanhood. At material level it consists of two kinds: *al-sadaqah al-tatawwu* given at the free will of the donor and *zakat*, the obligatory tax imposed by the Quran on the wealth of every Muslim having wealth beyond a certain limit.

ṣadaqah al-fiṭr (صدقة الفطر)

A small sum levied on all Muslims having income above a certain exemption level to be paid during the month of *Ramadan* to the poor people of the community. This *sadaqah* is obligatory and is an important part of the overall system of *sadaqat* in Islam.

al-ṣadaqah al-jāriyah (الصدقة الجارية)

A form of charity, benefits of which continue to accrue over generations, such as building a mosque, providing a well for drinking-water and constructing inns for travellers, etc. The range of *al-sadaqah al-jariyah* is very broad. The establishment of charitable trusts (*awqaf*) is an important example. Muslims have been exhorted by the Prophet to invest their wealth in *sadaqah al-jariyah* with rich promises of reward in the Hereafter. Spending on such acts carries a high value in Muslim society.

ṣadaqah al-najwah (صدقة النجوة)

Contribution required before seeking private consultation with the Prophet. This was made obligatory for a short time but abrogated subsequently.

ṣadaqah al-sawāʾim (صدقة السوائم)

Zakat on the grazing animal. See also *al-sawaim*.

al-sadaqāt al-wājibah (الصدقات الواجبة)

Compulsory charity such as *zakāt*, *sadaqah al-fitr*, etc. It also includes penal charity for such sins as breaking of oath, breaking of fast, etc.

al-sadīs (السديس)

Relating to the *nisab* of *zakat*, a camel in its eighth year.

al-ṣadūqah (الصدوقة)

Official designation for informal partnership during Fatimide and Ayubide Egypt.

al-safāhah (السفاهة)

Lit: Foolishness, imprudence. *Tech*: The quality of squandering wealth recklessly and against the spirit of the *shariah*. It includes *israf* and *tabdhir*. The quality of *safahah* invites the law of *hajr* by which the state can impose such restrictions on the utilization of assets as may be necessary to safeguard personal and social interests. One who has the quality of *safahah* is known as *al-safih* (plural, *sufaha*), which is the antonym of *al-rashid*. *Sufaha* include minor children, lunatics, extravagant persons and those who spend money to promote evil in the society. *See al-hajr* also.

al-safīh (السفيه)

See *al-safahah*.

al-ṣafīyah (الصفيه)
Share taken by the leader of an army before division of booty, such as horse or a sword. The term was later used as *sawafi* (singular, *safiya*) lands or possessions which the sultan (ruler) appropriated exclusively for himself. It also means all lands which their owners have abandoned or the owners of which have died leaving no heirs.

al-ṣafqah (الصفقة)
Lit: Striking of the hand of one person upon the hand of another in ratifying a sale or purchase and a covenant. It is also used to signify the contract that is itself made in the case of a sale.

ṣahib al-ʾashghāl (صاحب الأشغال)
Finance secretary in fourteenth century Muslim Spain. See also *musharrif*.

ṣāḥib bait al-māl (صاحب بيت المال)
See *bait al-mal*.

ṣāḥib al-ʿīnah (صاحب العينة)
In a contract of *bai al-inah*, the borrower.

ṣāḥib al-kharāj (صاحب الخراج)
An officer of the Muslim government responsible for the collection and administration of *al-kharaj*.

ṣāḥib al-maks (صاحب المكس)
Lit: Tax-collector. *Tech*: Tax-collector in the market who would take as tax more than what is due. Such a dishonest official has been condemned by the Prophet.

ṣāḥib al-māl (صاحب المال)
In a *mudarabah* contract, the person who provides the capital. See also *rabb al-mal*.

ṣāḥib al-niṣāb (صاحب النصاب)
Relating to the law of *zakat*, one who possesses wealth in excess of

the exemption-limit. Also used for one who possesses sufficient means to offer sacrifice or make the pilgrimage to Mecca. See also *nisab*.

ṣāhib al-sūq (صاحب السوق)

Lit: Guardian of the market. *Tech*: An alternate term for the *muhtasib* before the latter term gained currency.

al-sāʿī (الساعى)

Lit: The messenger. *Tech*: *Zakat*-collector who visits people at their places to collect the *zakat*.

saib al-bahr (سيب البحر)

Product of the sea, such as fish, amber and pearls. They are a free, natural gift and fall in the category of public property.

al-sāʾibah (السائبه)

A property that has been abandoned by its owner without transferring it to someone else.

sāʾīs (سائس)

Lit: Stableman. *Tech*: The person who used to collect *zakat* on cattle.

al-ṣakk (الصك)

Lit: Order of payment. *Tech*: The term was in vogue during the Muslim period. The *sakk* was a payment order on a banker with whom a person had an account.

salaf (سلف)

Lit: Advance payment, prepayment, free-loan, non-interest-bearing loan. *Tech*: It includes loans for specified periods, i.e. short, intermediate and long-term loans. But if it is to be paid on demand, it is called *qard*.

salam (سلم)

See *bai al-salam*.

al-samaḥah (السماحة)

Lit: Magnanimity, generosity. *Tech*: Spirit of beneficence in all commercial dealings, especially among debtors and creditors. It is an important economic value in a Muslim society. The Prophet has exhorted Muslims to forego part of the entire claim from a debtor if he becomes insolvent and to extend the period of payment if he is a victim of uneven circumstances. In other commercial dealings also the give-and-take should be done in a spirit of magnanimity.

al-sānīyah (السانية)

Lit: Water scoop. *Tech*: Water scoop fetched by camels. Produce of land irrigated by *saniyah* is subject to half-ushr (i.e. 5 per cent).

sard mursal (سرد مرسل)

A measure which conformed to an older authorized pattern. Imam Abu Yusuf recommended that the crop yield between landlord and tenant be distributed by using *sard mursal*. The emphasis seemed to be on the use of an authorized measure because it was nearer to justice.

al-ṣarf (الصرف)

See *bai al-sarf*.

al-sariqah (السرقة)

Lit: Theft. *Tech*: Taking away the property of another in a secret manner at a time when such property is in proper custody.

sāttuq dirham (ستوق درهم)

Lit: A coin without any redeeming quality. A coin of poor quality. *Tech*: Relating to the law of *mudarabah*, no valid agreement can take place with *sattuq dirhams*.

al-ṣawāfī (الصوافى)

Public estates belonging to the crown. They were also known as *diya al-ammah*. Income from them accrued to the *bait al-mal al-ammah*.

al-sawānī **(السوانى)**
Camels which work on wells to irrigate land. Half-ushr is levied on the produce of the land worked by *al-sawani*.

al-sawm **(السوم)**
Lit: Offer for sale (a commodity). *Tech*: It implies distracting a customer by offering a lower price or superior quality of an article; for instance, 2 persons might offer a certain commodity for a certain price, but another person might say, 'I can sell you the same thing for a lower price.' In modern language it implies to undersell a commodity or to dump goods at a lower price on the market.

SESRTCIC
See Statistical Economic and Social Research and Training Centre for Islamic Countries.

shafī' jār **(شفيع جار)**
A person, who owns an immovable property adjacent to the immovable property sold, has a right of pre-emption.

shafī' khalīṭ **(شفيع خليط)**
A participant in the immunities and appendages of immovable property sold, such as the right of passage, the right of passage of water or the right of irrigation.

shafī' sharīk **(شفيع شريك)**
A person who is a co-owner of some undivided immovable property with another person or persons.

shahnah **(شحنة)**
Relating to the administration of *iqta* in India of the sixteenth century A.D. The *shahnah* performed the functions of an amir who, instead of the *muqta* (assignee), governed the *khalissah* areas.

al-shaʿīrah (الشعيرة)
Lit: A grain of barley. *Tech*: Weight equivalent to 0.06 grams and a measure of length equivalent to 0.320 cm.

al-sharīʿah (الشريعة)
Lit: The way. *Tech*: The way of Allah as shown by the Quran and the sunnah of the Prophet. It is generally spoken to mean the Islamic law.

al-shibr (الشبر)
Lit: Span of the hand. *Tech*: A measure of length equal to 12 fingers, or 9 inches or 23.1 cm.

al-shirkah (الشركة)
A contract between two or more persons who launch a business or financial enterprise to make profits.

shirkah al-ʾabdān (شركة الأبدان)
Partnership between two or more persons in skill, mental or physical labour only (without capital). They accept work jointly, perform it according to their agreement and share the profit. This is also known as *shirkah al-sanaʾa*.

shirkah al-ʾamal (شركة العمل)
An alternate term for *shirkah al-abdan*.

shirkah al-ʾamwāl (شركة الأموال)
A contract of partnership where each partner brings in some capital in the shape of money and all the partners contribute their labour and skill, agreeing to share the profit.

shirkah al-ʿaqd (شركة العقد)
Lit: Contractual partnership. *Tech*: Two or more persons may continue to carry on business on the condition that the capital and the profit will be shared among them. This is distinguished from *shirkah al-mulk*, which is partnership in joint property.

al-shirkah bila-māl (الشركة بلامال)
An alternate term for *shirkah al-abdan*.

shirkah al-dhimam (شركة الذمم)
An association in which the communality consists of each partner sharing in the obligations incurred by his colleagues. This is a type of partnership in which partners do not invest any capital but instead authorize each other to buy on credit on the condition that each will be responsible for half the cost of the other's purchases and share in a like manner in the profit of their resale.

shirkah fil-ʿaml bi-ʾaidīhima (شركة فى العمل بأيديهما)
An alternate term for *shirkah al-abdān*.

shirkah al-jabr (شركة الجبر)
Partnership by compulsion exists if a purchaser purchases goods in the presence of a person who is a bonafide dealer in the particular commodity and the dealer has reason to believe that the goods are being purchased for him as usual. The bonafide dealer will be treated as a partner of the purchaser provided that the purchaser does not declare in anticipation to have purchased the goods for himself.

shirkah al-ʿinān (شركة العنان)
A partnership agreement in which the partners may have equal equity but unequal rights to profit, unequal equity with equal rights to profit or with unequal equity and unequal rights to profit.

shirkah al-mafālīs (شركة المفاليس)
Lit: Partnership of the penniless. *Tech*: It comes about when two or more people form a partnership without any capital to buy merchandise on credit and then sell it. Also known as *shirkah al-wujuh*.

shirkah al-milk (شركة الملك)
Lit: Proprietary partnership. *Tech*: A proprietary partnership occurs when two persons inherit or purchase something together. Neither of them is permitted to dispose off the other's portion

except with the other's permission. Each of them is considered a stranger in regard to the other's portion.

shirkah al-mufāwaḍah (شركة المفاوضة)
A contract of partnership in which all the partners are equal in respect of equity, and the right to conduct business for cash or credit. All of them are mutual agents and mutual sureties for one another.

shirkah al-sanā'a' (شركة الصنائع)
See *shirkah al-abdan*.

shirkah al-taḍāmun (شركة التضامن)
A contract of partnership among two or more partners who share the liabilities of the business created by any one of them.

Shirkah al-Takafol al-Islamiyya Bahrain (STI/Bahrain)
A subsidiary of DMI. Main objective is to conduct Islamic insurance business. Started operations in late 1984. Paid-up capital, US$10 million.

shirkah al-taqbīl (شركة التقبيل)
A form of *shirkah al-abdan* in which artisans join together in partnership on the condition that they would accept orders from customers concerning their trade and skill jointly and share income from the trade. It is also known as *shirkah al-taqabbul*.

shirkah al-tauṣīyah al-bāsiṭah (شركة التوصية الباسطة)
A partnership agreement in which one partner assumes unlimited liability of the business debt while the other partner remains liable to the extent of his own capital.

shirkah al-wujūh (شركة الوجوة)
Partnership between two or more persons carrying on business on credit only (without investment of capital). They purchase goods on credit on the basis of their goodwill and then sell them and try to make profit.

al-shufʿah (الشفعة)

Lit: Right of pre-emption. *Tech*: Acquiring a vendor's property at the price for which the vendor has sold it. The right of pre-emption is a power of possessing property which is for sale. It applies only to immovable property. It appertains in the first place to the co-sharer or partner in the property; secondly, to a sharer in the immunities and appendages of the property such as the right to water or to road; thirdly, to the neighbours.

al-shuḥḥ (الشح)

Lit: Stinginess, avarice. *Tech*: Petty-mindedness in inter-personal relationships. *Shuhh* leads one to selfishness, callousness and to disproportionate love for wealth.

al-shukr (الشكر)

Lit: Gratitude. *Tech*: A value of the Muslim society by virtue of which an individual acknowledges the bounties of Allah and expresses gratitude by tongue and actions, which are those actions one has been enjoined to carry out through obedience to Allah. It includes putting physical resources and faculties to their proper use. Their improper use contradicts *shukr* and is termed *kufr*.

al-siʿar al-maʿrūf (السعر المعروف)

See *thaman al-mithl*.

SIC

See *Specific Investment Certificates*.

SID

See *Specific Investment Deposits*.

al-sikkah (السكة)

Originally it meant a 'minting die' to test the fineness and weight of the coin. The same word subsequently came to be used for the mint as an office providing for and checking these marks.

al-silʿah (السلعة)
Commodity.

al-simsar (السمسار)
Lit: Middleman. *Tech*: One who sells on behalf of others.

specific investment certificates (SIC)
A proposed instrument of *riba*-free banking, the certificates offered by commercial banks to savers. These certificates would carry the name of an enterprise in which the value of the certificate would be invested. They would be exactly like stocks held by a member bank for a particular customer. The advantages include: use of bank's expertise and its block-vote as a representative of more than one stock holder.

specific investment deposits (SID)
Proposed financial instrument of *riba*-free economy. Indicates deposits with commercial banks with specific purposes and defined maturities.

specific muḍārabah
A *mudarabah* contract with one specific purpose or objective.

Statistical Economic and Social Research and Training Centre for Islamic Countries (SESRICIC)
Founded in 1978 and based at Ankara, the centre, in co-operation with the IDB, Jeddah, and the Turkish Institute for Statistics is supposed to expand into a data bank in which all data relevant to economic policy in the Islamic world are available. The centre performs policy oriented studies for experts and ministerial meetings of which a number have appeared in the *Journal for Economic Co-operation among Islamic Countries*, published by the centre since 1979.

al-suʿāt (السعاة)
Zakat-collectors, especially on animals and on agricultural property.

sūd (urdu)
Lit: Gain or profit. *Tech*: Interest on capital borrowed. It has been used interchangeably with *riba* in Urdu literature on Islamic economics and *fiqh*.

al-suftajah (السفتجة)
Tech: A type of banking instrument used for the delegation of credit during the Muslim period, especially by the Abbasides. It was used to collect taxes, disburse government dues and transfer funds by merchants. It was the most important banking instrument used by traveller merchants. In some cases *suftajahs* were payable at a future fixed date and in other cases they were payable on sight. *Suftajah* is distinct from the modern bill of exchange in some respects. Firstly, a sum of money transferred by *suftajah* had to keep its identity and payment to be made in the same currency. Exchange of currencies could not take place in this course. Secondly, *suftajah* usually involved three persons: 'A' pays a certain sum of money to 'B' for agreeing to give an order to 'C' to pay it back to 'A'. Third, a *suftajah* could be endorsed. The Arabs had been using endorsements (*hawalah*) since the days of the Prophet. See also *al-tamassuk*.

al-suḥbah (الصحبة)
Official designation for informal business co-operation or 'companionship' during Fatimide and Ayubide Egypt. Merchants of lesser stature were known as *sahib* or *companion* of a merchant or firm of greater reputation.

ṣulḥ-fai' (صلح فیء)
The *mal* which returns to Muslims without fighting from the enemies. It is not divided among Muslims as is *anwa-fai*, which is obtained by fighting and divided among the warriors as war booty. See also *ghanimah*.

al-sunnah (السنن)
Lit: Custom, habit, way of life. *Tech*: Utterances of the Prophet other than the Quran, known as ahadith, or his personal acts, or acts and sayings of others tacitly approved by him.

al-swā'im (السوائم)
Lit: Pasturing animals. *Tech*: Those animals which are bred and pastured that they may grow. It excludes animals kept for riding, for work or for carrying of loads.

T

al-ta'āwun (التعاون)
Lit: Co-operation. *Tech*: *al-taawun* is a basic principle of economic enterprise in Islam. The various relationships between customer and merchant, capitalist and consumer, labourer and enterpreneur, and among individuals, institutions and the state are based on the concept of co-operation and not on conflict.

al-tabarru' (التبرع)
Lit: Gift, donation. *Tech*: Relating to the law of *mufawadah* partnership, it means the right of complete and unfettered disposition over joint property. This right has not been conceded by the jurists to any partner. However, one has the right of *tabarru* with personal property. See *al-tasarruf*.

al-tabdhīr (التبذير)
Lit: To squander, waste or dissipate. *Tech*: Spending on objects which have been explicitly prohibited by the *shariah* irrespective of the quantum of expenditure.

al-tabī' (التبيع)
Relating to the *nisab* of *zakat*, a one-year-old calf of the cow.

al-tabkhīs (التبخيس)
To decrease the quality or quantity of a product offered for sale at the original price.

Tadamun Islamic Bank Sudan (TIB/SUDAN)
Incorporated on 24 March 1983. Besides the head office, there are nine branches in Sudan. Authorized capital, US$50 million. Paid-up capital, US$13.4 million.

al-tadlīs (التدليس)

Tech: Hiding the defects of a commodity from its potential buyers.

al-taḥjīr (التحجير)

Lit: To build a stone-fence, a wall or something similar on land. *Tech*: To clear rocks off the land, levelling the ground, building water canals, pulling out weeds and irrigating.

al-tājir al-muqim (التاجر المقيم)

A resident merchant. See *al-tajir al-saffar*.

al-tājir al-saffār (التاجر السفار)

During mediaeval times, a merchant who travelled in connection with his business. The Muslim merchants travelled along ocean and land routes with merchandise. See *al-tajir al-muqim*.

al-takāfu' (التكافوأ)

Lit: Equality. *Tech*: Principle of proportionality in the Maliki law of partnership, requiring the distribution of profit and liability to correspond to various components of investment.

al-takāful (التكافل)

Lit: Mutual or joint responsibility. *Tech*: Mutual support which is the basis of the concept of insurance or solidarity among Muslims. Not institutionalized, it is a broad concept and covers a much wider area than *zakat*, which is an instance of *takaful*. If one waives a debt when the debtor is unable to pay, this is an example of *takaful* but not necessarily of *zakat*. It is also the name of an insurance with investment instrument launched by DMI.

al-takāthur (التكاثر)

Lit: Plenty, abundance. *Tech*: In the Quran (102:1), the word is used to mean one's obsession with worldly possessions, with wealth, strength, position and the like, things that make people selfish and forgetful of their duties to God and to fellow beings.

al-takhriṣ (التخريص)
An alternate term for *khars*.

al-takmilah (التكملة)
Relating to the fiscal law of mediaeval Islam, it refers to additional charges on the landholders who stayed in a village to make up for the payment of those who deserted the land or died. This was a consequence of collective assessment of land tax.

talaqqi al-jalab (تلقى الجلب)
One of the commercial practices of early Arabia. Traders would, on hearing of a merchandise caravan, proceed out of the city to meet the caravan, to buy the entire merchandise and bring it to the city to sell at monopolistic and exploitative prices.

al-talji'ah. (التلجئة)
Lit: Refuge, shelter. *Tech*: Common in Iraq of Umayyad and Abbaside, it refers to circumstances of a weak person commiting his land to the protection of a strong citizen against foreign troops, bandits or government tax-collectors. This was also known as *himayah* or *khafarah*. The feudal lord would collect tax from the person seeking *taljiah* who acted as a *muzara*. This tax often covered government dues plus the feudal lord's share for providing protection. Such *'ilja* lands were often annexed by the government and distributed among the courtiers. The government always felt threatened by the power of the feudal lords but had to live with this evil.

al-tamakkun (التمكن)
Lit: Power, authority, ability. *Tech*: Quranic usage for political stability and economic prosperity. Economic development without political solidarity is not conceivable. Therefore, *al-tamakkun* may be an alternative term for economic progress and stability.

al-tamassuk (التمسك)
Lit: A written commitment. *Tech*: I.O.U., a credit document. It is also known as *al-suftajah*.

al-tamlīk **(التمليك)**

Lit: To make someone the owner of property. *Tech*: Used in the context of *zakat*. The Hanafite school of jurisprudence contends that the only legal form of *zakat* expenditure is the transfer of funds to poor persons so that it becomes the property of those people. The implication of this condition is that *zakat* cannot be used for purposes where such personal transfer of funds is not possible.

al-tanā'ah **(التناء)**

See *al-tunna*.

al-tanājush **(التناجش)**

Lit: Concealment, rousing and chasing the game for the purpose of snaring it. *Tech*: In business transactions, this term means to demand the sale of an article of merchandise for more than its price, not meaning to purchase but only to ensnare the innocent buyer. It is also known as *bai al-najash*.

al-tana'um **(التنعم)**

Indulgence in luxuries, a mode of behaviour discouraged by Islam.

al-tanḍīḍ **(التنضيض)**

Lit: Derived from *nadd*, which means hard cash. *Tech*: Relating to a contract of *mudarabah*, it refers to liquidation of all real assets immediately before calculating the profit.

tapu

The Turkish system of granting lands to the cultivators introduced by the law of 1858. The *miri* lands were granted directly to cultivators together with a title deed or *tapu*. The holder of a *tapu* was entitled to cultivate the land as he pleased, and was free to pledge or alienate it provided he received the express permission of the state. On his death the land passed on to his lawful heirs without the necessity for a new *tapu* to be granted. If the possessor died without heirs, the land passed to the inhabitants of the village to which he belonged. The permission of the state was also necessary before the holder could build houses or plant trees on his land. In return, the holder was obliged to make a payment to the government at the time of the original grant and was also liable to the rule of the shariah whereby the holder was dispossesed if the land remained uncultivated for three years.

al-taraf (الترف)
Lit: Indulgence in luxuries. *Tech*: Pride, arrogance and disregard for proper rules of conduct caused by possession and enjoyment of worldly riches. See *rafah*.

al-taṣarruf (التصرف)
Relating to the law of partnership, it means the partners' freedom to dispose off joint property within the contractual framework. See *al-tabarru*.

al-tassabub (التسبب)
See *al-hawalah*

al-tasāwum (التساوم)
See *al-sawm*.

al-tasbīl (التسبيل)
An alternate term for *al-waqf*.

al-tasʿīr (التسعير)
Lit: To regulate prices. *Tech*: The power of the state to fix, control or determine the prices of goods in the market. It also includes regulation of profit, wages and rents by the state.

tasʿīru alʾ-ujrah (تسعير الأجرة)
Fixing of wages for labour in the private sector by the state.

al-tashrīk (التشريك)
An alternate term for *al-muzarah*.

al-ṭasq (الطسق)
Tax levied on different cereals on the basis of land measurement. Also a tax levied on newly created opportunity.

al-taṣriyah (التصرية)
See *al-musarrah*.

al-ṭassūj (الطسوق)
A weight measuring ¼ *daniq*, equivalent to 0.1247 grams.

al-taswīyah (التسوية)
Lit: Equality. *Tech*: The basic principle of distribution of *fai* followed by Abu Bakr. He distributed the *fai* at an equal rate among all.

al-taṭfīf (التطفيف)
Lit: Weighing short.

al-tawḥīd (التوحيد)
Lit: Oneness of God. *Tech*: God is one and does not share anything with anybody, neither in personality nor qualities. Belief in *tawhid* is fundamental to Islam, and the value system of Islam is based on this belief. It affects the economic behaviour of Muslims in a number of ways.

tawkīl al-iqraḍ (توكيل الإقراض)
Lit: Authorization to lend. *Tech*: Authorization to lend cash in a contract of *mudarabah* for the *mudarib* or the working partners.

tawkīl al-istiqrāḍ (توكيل الإستقراض)
Lit: Authorization for raising a loan. *Tech*: In a contract of *mudarabah* or *shirkah*, the *rabbul mal* or the other partners may authorize the *mudarib* or working partner to raise a loan in cash for the business over and above the capital.

al-tawqīʿ (التوقيع)
Lit: Signature. *Tech*: A banking instrument of the mediaeval Muslim period: a payment order to draw money from a bank.

al-tauẓīf (التوظيف)
Lit: Employment. *Tech*: Appointment of a person to collect *kharaj* or to undertake trade.

al-tawakkul (التوكل)
Lit: Trust, confidence. *Tech*: Trust in God for results after one has provided all material resources. It also means confidence in the help from God in all matters, one of the important values in a Muslim society. It is often confused by Western observers with fatalism and thought to be one of the causes of under-development of Muslim countries but its real significance is just the opposite. It invites fearless efforts to explore all avenues in the hope that God's help shall come. *Al-tawakkul* inculcates enterprise rather than fatalism.

al-tawarruq (التورق)
A sales contract in which the buyer obtains merchandise on credit and then sells it at a loss to another person for cash. The purpose of such a transaction is to get cash and not to do business. It is condemned as a trick to give or to get an interest-bearing loan.

al-ṭayyibāt (الطيبات)
Lit: Good things, good and pure things. *Tech*: Used in the Quran for the consumer's goods provided to human beings. The concept carries with it man's responsibilities to God and other human beings for the use of these good things. It excludes the *haram* goods from its domain.

al-thaman (الثمن)
Lit: Price, cost, value. *Tech*: Price of an article as agreed by the buyer and the seller in a contract of sale. (It may be different from the prevalent market price.)

al-thaman al-ʿājil (الثمن العاجل)
The sale price of a commodity which is paid in cash at the time of a sale deed.

thaman al-mithl (الثمن المثل)
Prevalent price in the market. Relating to the concept of *tasir*, *al-thaman al-mithl* is enforced by the state in case someone unjustly charges a higher price.

al-thamanīyah
Moneyed, regarded by many jurists as the *illah* (basis of prohibition) of *riba al-fadl* applied to gold and silver. Hence, the same prohibition is applied to paper currency.

al-thimārah al-bāqiyyah (الثمارة الباقية)
Relating to the law of *zakat*, fruits which do not rot for a major part of the year without artificial conditioning.

thanīyyu (الثنى)
Tech: Relating to the law of *zakat*, it refers to a lamb of one year, a cow of two years or a camel of five years. It is also referred to as *thaniyyah*.

al-tibr (التبر)
Lit: Metal ore, gold dust, gold nuggets. *Tech*: Relating to the law of *zakat*, gold or silver not cast into ornaments or utensils.

al-tijārah al-ghā'ibah (التجارة الغائبة)
Lit: Absent trade. *Tech*: Long distance trade or trade in a town other than the one in which a trader resides. See also *al-tijarah al-hadirah*.

al-tijārah al-ḥāḍirah (التجارة الحاضرة)
Lit: Present trade. *Tech*: Local trade, also used for day-to-day dealings among businessmen. It is not necessary to record the credit transactions in such cases. See *al-tijarah al-ghaibah*.

al-timār (التيمار)
See *ard al-timar*.

al-tirāzah (الترازة)

Lit: A device made use of in a sluice that distributes water in definite standard units according to the common agreement of the owners and according to their rights. *Tech: al-Tirazah* was employed as a method in the assessment of *al-misahah* in the Abbaside period. It was a method of making an equitable assessment of tax, keeping in view fertility of the soil, its facility for irrigation and the category of its crop.

al-tu'mah (الطعمة)

Lit: Food grant. *Tech*: Entitlement to receive food grant from a piece of land during one's lifetime. For example, from the lands of Fadak, the Prophet and his family were entitled to a food grant during his lifetime, after which these lands reverted to the *bait al-māl*.

al-tunnā' (التناء)

A class of landlords during the Abbaside period, who were mostly absentee landlords, leaving management of their estates to their deputies. They often acted as contractors for tax collection and their riches accrued more from this latter activity. They were also known as *al-tanaah*.

U

'ukhuwah (أخوة)

Lit: Brotherhood, fraternity. *Tech*: The interrelationships of Muslims in the society are regulated by a sense of *ukhuwah*. It is the basis of mutual benevolence in the society. Some of the economic relations are also governed by *ukhuwah*.

al-'umrā (العمرى)

Grant of land or property by state or by an individual free of cost, along with rights of ownership. *Al-umra* are unencumbered grants, which the descendants of the grantee inherit as any other property. But in certain cases the donor may condition its use by the donee during the latter's life-time. In such a case the gift is inherited by the donor and his heirs and is not passed on to the heirs of the donee.

'ūqīyah **(اوقية)**
Lit: A weight of varying magnitude. *Tech*: Equivalent to 40 dirhams or 119.07 grams. It is known as *uqiyah al-fiddah* in distinction to *uqiyah al-ashya*, which is equal to 7.5 dirhams or 23.782 grams.

'ūqīyah al-'āshyā' **(اوقية الأشياء)**
See *uqiyah*.

'ūqīyah al-fīḍḍah **(اوقية الفضة)**
See *uqiyah*.

al-'ūrf **(العرف)**
Relating to the sources of Islamic law, it is the customs and the usages of a particular society.

al-'urūd **(العروض)**
Lit: Merchandise, stock-in-trade. *Tech*: Jurists apply this term in different connotations: (a) sometimes it is applied to everything except cash; (b) sometimes it is applied to everything except cash, eatables, garments and immovable property; (c) sometimes it is applied to everything except cash, measurables, weighables, animals and immovable property.

al-'ushr **(العشر)**
Lit: One-tenth. *Tech*: A tax on the agricultural produce of lands levied only on Muslims at the rate of 10 per cent if the land is irrigated by rainfall and at the rate of 5 per cent on the artificially-irrigated lands. *Ushr* is not levied, if there is no produce. It is also known as *zakah al-ard*. The *zakat* is levied on moveable property if it remains in one's possession for one year, but the *ushr* is payable on each crop. The *ushr* is payable on the produce of the land even if the owner is a minor or a lunatic. The ownership of land

is not a condition for *ushr* because it is payable on *waqf* lands as well as on the produce of the land being tilled under a contract of *muzarah*. It is levied on the gross produce. The cost of the produce is not accounted for prior to the assessment of the *ushr*. The *ushr* revenues are usually spent on those accounts on which the *zakat* is spent. See also *al-Zakah*.

al-ʿushūr (العشور)

Lit: One-tenth. *Tech*: *al-ushur* were imposed on the merchants who came to Muslim lands from non-Muslim countries which had no treaty with Muslims. Eventually, *al-ushur* were extended to all the caravans, whether for internal or external trade, and to Muslim and non-Muslim merchants. For a Muslim merchant, *ushur* were the same as 2.5 per cent annual *zakat* on merchandise. A *dhimmi* had to pay double what a Muslim paid, whereas a merchant from a foreign country which had no relations with Muslims had to pay double what a *dhimmi* paid. It used to be an important source of revenue for the Muslim state.

V

VAP (value-added participation)

This concept has been given by some economists to replace PLS as a basis for Islamic banking. It is contended that VAP would be nearer to justice and would give greater stability to the profits of the banks. However, it's permissibility under the shariah is doubtful, because under this concept the bank would be able to get a return in any case. The value-added participation means that the bank would provide funds for a business on the condition that the bank would get a fixed percentage of the value-added as a return. The value-added would be calculated by (a) gross turnover less purchases and services, or (b), wages, salaries and pensions plus interest on capital plus taxes plus dividends plus depreciation plus retained profits. Thus, value-added can never be a negative figure. The bank would always get a return. The concept has only changed the predetermined rate of interest to a variable rate of interest.

W

waḍʿ al-jawāʾiḥ (وضع الجوائح)

The amount of discount or commission which a landlord is required to grant to the tenant in case some calamity befalls the crop and the tenant is put to abnormal loss. The Prophet instructed to grant a proportionate concession in rent to such an unfortunate tiller of the land.

al-waḍīʿah (الوضعية)

Resale of goods with a discount on the original stated cost.

al-waḍāʾiʿ (الوضائع)

A comprehensive term expressing all taxes.

al-wadīyah (الوديعة)

Lit: Deposit, trust. *Tech*: A contract whereby a person leaves valuables as a trust for safe-keeping.

al-wadīʿyah bil ʾajr (الوديعة بالأجر)

Lit: Deposit for fee. *Tech*: A form of contract where a person deposits a sum with another person on payment of a fee for safe keeping, with permission for the trustee to make use of the amount if needed. The trustee is held responsible for any loss in the amount deposited.

al-waibah (الويبة)

A dry measure equal to 5.5 *sa*, prevalent in early Muslim Egypt. According to Hanafites, it is equivalent to 17.938 kg or 18.491 litres, whereas other jurists consider it equivalent to 11.946 kg or 15.114 litres.

al-wakālah (الوكالة)

Lit: Representation, agency. *Tech*: Contract of agency in which a person delegates his business to another and substitutes the other in his own place. The latter is called the *wakil*, or agent, and the former is called *muwakkil*, or principal.

al-waqf (pl. al-awqāf) (الوقف)

Lit: Detention. *Tech*: Appropriation or tying up of a property in perpetuity so that no proprietary rights can be exercised over the corpus but only over the usufruct. The *waqf* property can neither be sold nor inherited or donated to anyone. *al-awqaf* consisted of religious foundations set up for the benefit of the poor. Conceived in such a way, the administration of the *waqf*, together with the salary that it involved, was often reserved for the founder and his family until the founder's line of descent became extinct. They were often set up as an indirect way of avoiding too strict a division of the property under the terms of the law of succession, retaining it for the male members of the family in undivided form.

al-waqf al-'ahlī (الوقف الأهلى)

Private trusts instituted for the benefit of family members. See also *al-waqf*.

al-waqf al-'āmm (الوقف العام)

Public endowment set apart for a charitable or religious purpose.

al-waqf 'ala al-'awlād (الوقف عل الاولاد)

An endowment for the family of the donor. Its proceeds accrue to the members of the donor's family and after the death of the last descendant of the donor, it reverts to the *bait al-mal*. It is also known as *al-waqf al-dhurri* or *al-waqf al-khass*.

al-wāqf al-dhūrrī (الوقف الذرى)

See *al-waqf ala al-awlad*.

al-waqf al-khairī (الوقف الخيرى)

Waqf for the general good, intented to fulfil a noble social function, especially in respect of those functions that have not been performed by the state such as hospitals, schools, asylums, public water supply, cemeteries and mosques. See also *al-waqf*.

al-waqṣ (pl. al-ʾawqāṣ) (الوقص)

Lit: The broken (number). *Tech*: Relating to the law of *zakat* on cattle. The slab rates of *zakat* on cattle proceed with the series 10, 20, 30, 40, etc., in multiples of ten. Any figure lying between the two limits (i.e. lower and upper limits) is known as *awqas*. For example, cattle numbering more than 30 but fewer than 40 are known as *awqas*.

al-waṣiyyah (الوصية)

Lit: Bequest or will. *Tech*: A transfer to come into operation after the testator's death. The testator is called *musi*, the legatee is called *musalahu* and the executor is called *wasi*.

al-wasq (الوسق)

Lit: Load, freight, cargo. *Tech*: A measure of weight; one *wasq* = 60 *sa*. According to Hanafites, it is equivalent to 192.69 kg or 201.72 litres, while other jurists consider it equivalent to 130.32 kg or 164.88 litres.

al-waẓīfah (الوظيفة)

Lit: Pay, daily ration. *Tech*: (a) A pension or stipend granted to pious persons. (b) Revenue collected at a stipulated rate and time. Sometimes used in the sense of a supplementary tax in addition to *jizyah*. See also *al-kharaj al-wazifah*.

wiqāyah al-ʿirḍ (وقاية العرض)

Lit: Protection of honour. *Tech*: Spending on people to protect one's honour. For example, giving something to poets, slanderers or enemies to keep them away so that they do not indulge in defamation.

Y

al-yamīn al-ghamūs (اليمين الغموس)

Lit: An oath which may land one in disaster. *Tech*: A false oath made in order to appropriate the property of someone else unlawfully. Such an oath is called *al-ghamus*, since it takes its bearer to the fire of Hell.

Z

al-zakāh (zakat) (الزكاة)

Lit: To purify. *Tech*: A tax which is levied on all persons having wealth above an exemption limit at a rate fixed by the *shariah* to purify wealth and souls from impure love. The object is to take away a part of the wealth of the well-to-do and to distribute it to the poor and the needy. It is levied on cash, cattle, agricultural produce, minerals, capital invested in industry and business, etc. The distribution of *zakat* fund has been laid down in the Quran (9:60) and is for the poor, the needy, *zakat*-collectors, new Muslims, travellers when in difficulty, the way of God, captives and debtors.

The *zakat* is payable if the owner is a Muslim and sane person. The *zakat* is the third pillar of Islam. The term *sadaqah* also occurs in the Quran and incorporates *zakat*. The *al-sadaqah* is of two kinds: *sadaqah tatawu* (voluntary contribution) and *sadaqah mafrudah* (obligatory contribution). In the terminology of *fiqh*, a clear distinction between *sadaqah* and *zakat* is made, since *sadaqah* generally refers to any kind of charity which is given for the sake of God. The *zakat* signifies the obligatory contribution which every well-off muslim has to pay to the Islamic state, in the absence of which individuals are required to distribute the *zakat* among its beneficiaries. See also *al-ushr*.

zakāh al-'ain (زكاة العين)

Zakat on cash, ornaments, gold or silver.

zakāh al-'arḍ (زكاة الارض)

An alternate term for *ushr*.

zakāh al-ghallat (زكاة الغلات)
Lit: *Zakat* on agricultural produce. *Tech: Ushr* or one-tenth of the agricultural produce paid out as a tithe.

zakāh al-hubūb (زكاة الحبوب)
Lit: *Zakat* on cereals.